I Hope Someone:
A Womanist Response to Spiritual and Psychological Trauma

Dr. Desjamebra J. Robinson

©2017

Revised Edition 2019

Rochester, NY

ISBN: 9781792634864

To My Sista,
Dr. Nicole —
I hope this helps you help
someone else.
Let Your light Shine Always.
Dr. D. Robinson
2019

Table of Contents

Abstract:

This work is a womanist theological perspective in response to the causes and effects of spiritual and psychological disorientation due to the trauma of Childhood Sexual Abuse (CSA). I will refer to this spiritual and psychological condition as Trauma-based Psycho-Spiritual Disorientation (TbPSD). My claim is that understanding the various facets of Trauma- based Psycho-Spiritual Disorientation will contribute to a deeper understanding of the necessity of worship especially for women of color.

The goal of this study is to acknowledge specific psychological conditions, spiritual and behavioral responses that manifest in the life of women of color post-trauma and apply womanist theological solution of worship. Womanist theory and theology will assist this work by providing a different point of view as it relates to trauma.

This work will help its readers gain insight about the stress of living with psychological and spiritual disorientation due to the trauma of Childhood Sexual Abuse. It will also bring attention to the significant correlation of Childhood Sexual Abuse and Domestic Violence (D.V.). It is my goal to present definitions and terms relevant to the work so that the reader may gain a clear understanding of what Trauma-based Psycho-Spiritual Disorientation is as a treatable/curable disease.

The target of this dissertation is to reveal some of the recognizable response behaviors of a woman dealing with the aftereffects of traumatization and provide some philosophical and theological reasoning for those responses. As a result, the readers of this work will grasp an awareness of the necessity for corporate worship to include women of color. The targeted areas of awareness include the physical, psychological, and pneumatic (spiritual) perceptions of the self and others within the Postmodern Urban Church. This includes acknowledging both the identity of the person sitting in the pews, and the identity of the Church as a whole.

This study does not promise to provide or substitute a cure to women of color who are currently dealing with the effects of Trauma-based Psycho-spiritual Disorientation. The information provided here is not to replace professional therapy for psychological illnesses. This work simply provides logic, concepts, and experiences that may help to shape and affirm individual paths to spiritual and psychological wellness.

Overview:

Chapter One: Womanist Theology Overview:
This chapter offers a brief overview of womanist theology and its significance to this research and work. It is important to understand the significance of theology for women of color, and its contribution to their social identity and theological location within the church. This chapter offers a brief historical view of womanism, which lays a foundation to understanding the necessity of worship for women of color.

Chapter Two: The Broken Pew
This chapter involves an analysis of the postmodern church and the way it responds to trauma caused by domestic violence such as Childhood Sexual Abuse, abandonment and physical battering. I will talk about the emotional stresses of devastation, destruction, and division, which destroy communication among families and communities. Next, I will use a scriptural example of how the spirit of a victim of abuse is broken due to the improper handling of their situation by family members, and also by the impulses of others within their community. I will introduce the concept of Psycho-Spiritual Disorientation due to trauma and its contribution to unresolved issues. Lastly, I will introduce the need for

lament by revisiting the background story of our woman sitting in the broken pew in the rear of the postmodern church, concluded by a Womanist sermon I wrote for her.

Chapter Three: Broken Pews and Broken People
This chapter deals with statistical data pertaining to the cause and effect of domestic violence, featuring a focus on its traumatic effects on society. It also highlights the systems that interconnect with them, such as mental health care and abortion clinics. In this section, we will identify broken pews and broken people—those sitting in the broken pews of the church and their relationship with domestic violence. This chapter will highlight the need for effective responses to those who have experienced victimization and abuse. This chapter will examine the correlation of abuse, domestic violence, Childhood Sexual Abuse, and its contributions to abnormal behaviors and identity disorders.

Major contributions to this work are perspectives by Phyllis Trible, Abraham Maslow's *Hierarchy of Needs Theory*, and Eric Erikson's *Stages of Psychosocial Development*. This is a psychoanalytic theory which identifies eight stages through which a healthily developing human should pass from infancy to late adulthood. In each stage, the person confronts, and hopefully masters, new challenges. Each stage builds upon the successful completion of earlier stages. The challenges of stages not successfully completed may be expected to reappear as problems in the future. It will involve the use of Maslow's theory of self-actualization coupled with Carl Rogers' theory of growth potential.[i] Ann Olson says "Maslow's hierarchy reflects a linear pattern of growth depicted in a direct pyramidal order of ascension. Moreover, he states that self-actualizing individuals are able to resolve dichotomies such as that reflected in the seemingly contrary concepts of free-will and determinism. He also contends that self-actualizers are highly creative, psychologically robust individuals. It is argued herein that a dialectical transcendence of ascension toward self-actualization better describes this type of self-actualization, and even the mentally ill, whose psychopathology correlates with creativity, have the capacity to self-actualize."

Chapter Four: Balancing the Books

The chapter titled *"Balancing the Books"* deals with the process of reconciling and the result of reconciliation. This chapter will deal with revisiting, reflecting, and resolving. There I will continue the conversation from chapter one, focusing on the process of forgiveness. I will illustrate how physical dynamics such as domestic violence and abuse, which cause physical trauma, also affect the psychological wellness of an individual. In consideration of the woman in the broken pew, and with an aim to help other individuals in defining where they are in their current developmental stage of life, I will identify the stages where trauma has occurred and identify a path of remedy. Identity will be a theme throughout this study.

Chapter Five: Worship is Therapeutic

In Chapter five, I will present a Womanist theological view responding to the need of the woman who entered the average postmodern urban church and sat down in the broken pew. This woman's journey is weaved throughout this dissertation. The chapter highlights that she and the church must be invited into an understanding of an all-inclusive approach to begin the process of administering the treatment and cure for Trauma-Based Psycho-Spiritual Disorientation. The remedies, for women of color are in the authentic worship experience. This chapter will explain worship and preaching as consubstantial therapeutic articulations of suffering, as well as being theocentric and therapeutic methods women may use to communicate lament and praise.

Chapter Six: Words of Encouragement and Conclusive Thoughts

Chapter six is a summative chapter which includes a letter of encouragement to the woman sitting in a broken pew. In addition, I have added a few sermons that I would preach to this woman to give her a perspective on how to heal. In addition, the sermons are shaped in a way to minister not only to women, but also to the men who are and should be included in the conversations.

A Background Story

Unresolved Issues:

When she was eight years old, she knew in her heart and in her soul that she loved God. She went to church every Sunday, with her grandparents. Her grandfather was the preacher. He would preach God's Word so clearly and plainly, that every time he invited the congregation to the altar for a call to salvation, she stood up to receive it. Of course, at eight years old, she did not know what she would need to be saved from, but she knew she wanted to be saved by God and the power of Jesus. Her grandparents would pick her up for church. She loved Jesus, she loved the Word of God, and she loved the Bible. She loved her brother, and she loved going to church.

It was at age eight, her world began to fall apart. Her parents married when she was five years old, and her baby brother was born right before her eighth birthday. Something changed in her relationship with her family: her father began molesting her. Her parents were fighting more, and the police were always at the house. Eventually, her father was removed from the home due to the frequency of domestic violence. Her mother moved their residency frequently with her and her brother, and they were often left alone often because of their mother's drug addiction. The two things this little girl wanted to protect the most were her brother and her faith.

After abandonment by their mother and the intervention of child protective services, she and her younger brother were placed with their father. At age 11, her father used her love for Jesus and the Word of God to manipulate for his own pleasure. He used her love for God's Word and showed her the story of Lot, telling her about how his daughters slept with him to save his life.[ii] He told her that he was dying of prostate cancer, and that it was her responsibility to save his life by allowing him to have sex with her. He used a biblical narrative to manipulate his daughter. She loved her father, and she believed that since it was in the Bible, it had to have been right. Of course, her father would not lie to her; he loved her, right?

One evening, after her grandparents had dropped her off home from church, her father approached her for sex. His mind was fixed on satisfying his worldly desires at the expense of those under his control. As he followed her to her room, she shouted at him, "In the name of Jesus," she said, "leave me alone!" She went into her room and shut the door. Her father was not pleased with the rebuke. Her rebuke was a spiritual response to a spiritual problem.

The following week, when it was time for her grandparents to pick her up for church she was not allowed to go. While the father could not defeat her spiritual authority, he used his positional power over her as her father to oppress her and weaken her spirit. He often said that she was on punishment, because of her behavior.

The psychological abuse got worse. It was no longer this manipulative tactic suppressing her. Her father had become a shadow of oppression. He made sure to surveillance very move she made, every phone conversation, and every friend she had. He was oppressing her physically, psychologically and spiritually. She was failing in school, because she could not concentrate on the work. She was fighting a lot. She fought not only in the physical realm, but also in the spiritual realms against her father.

As she got older in her teen years the abuse continued. Her father continued sexually abusing her, using his positional power in her life to oppress her and maintain his abuse. When his manipulation did not work, he punished her severely, isolated her, if she resisted him, he hit her.

When her parents briefly reconciled, her mother resented her because the father had abused her. The mother was jealous of the teenage girl. It seemed like every opportunity her mother had, she verbally and physically abused the girl. She called her names like "bitch," "hoe," and "stupid." One phrase that repeated in her mind was when her mother taunted her and said to her, "that's why your daddy is fucking you; you little bitch!" The mother not only blamed the girl for the abuse, she mocked the girl for the abuse she was enduring. It was as though she expected the pre-teen to have more control of what was happening to her. Rather than comforting her daughter the mother withheld love, and instead challenged her as though she were her 32-year-old equal; but the girl was only 13 years old.

Every emotional strike she received came not only from her father, but now from both her parents. She was being injured at one of the most vulnerable times in her life- on every level of her development; physiologically, psychologically and spiritually. While her parents were seemingly careful not to leave any physical scars, and some of the bruises healed—the spiritual and emotional wounds remained- and were left unattended.

Her mother abandoned her and her brother a second time; and this time love for her mother shriveled into a deep-seated anger. Resentment began to set in. She was 15 years old and still struggling to maintain her identity and connection to God. She needed strength to protect her brother, but she did not know how or where she would get it. As she grew older her father began to physically abuse her. He hit her more often because she refused him sexual encounters.

She found a way to survive. When she could not take the abuse, oppression, and manipulation any more she told the authorities. After she told the authorities what her father had been doing to her, she joined the military so that she could take care of her brother. She would have to leave her baby brother behind for a while. She risked perpetuating the effects of abandonment and psychological trauma to him because of the dysfunction of their family.

The plan failed. The police arrested her father, child protective services placed her brother with her mother, and she had to testify against her father in a trial with the courts. With this failed attempt at becoming stable in the military, she returned home to depression, which led to drug addiction and incarceration. Her walk on this road of life was as though a jackhammer had been let loose and allowed to plow and dig random holes in her state of mind. These holes were like pockets of shattered stones and gravel. Every time it rained in her life; these holes would fill up in the wells of her eyes leaving muddy puddles behind.

Unresolved Issue: A Theological View

Spiritual and psychological oppression without recourse is frustrating for anyone. But, especially for women in general due to the years of being ignored by their male counterparts. According to the *New Bible Commentary*, the story of Lot and his two daughters portrays a "pathetic end to a righteous man who had compromised with the world."[iii] This story shows the perpetuation of dysfunctionality within a family dynamic. It shows how manipulation is a powerful tool for twisted views to preserve themselves and permeate throughout a generation and embed themselves into a culture. Lot's family shows repeated displays of putting their worldly desires of self-preservation—influenced by the culture surrounding them—ahead of their moral and spiritual values.[iv] They had broken the rules about incest and filial duty.[v] Their concepts and ideas came from the temptation of sin influenced by the worldly cultures around them, living in Sodom. Surprisingly, in the *Women's Bible Commentary*, there is no reference to this portion of this story.[vi] When it comes to this story, theologians and commentary writers have failed to address the story effectively. Maybe this is because there is nowhere to pinpoint the blame for the mindset of this family.

The blame may lie in the immediate cultural influence, explained by the psychology of temptation surrounding them. Consider the absent mother, who pursued her own self-gratification by maintaining her attachment to the culture of Sodom. The father that was willing to permit men in the community to rape his daughters, simply to protect his status with strangers. Imagine the psychological mindset of his daughters who, after escaping the destruction of Sodom and Gomorrah, maintained a level of low self-esteem and cultural attachment to participate in the behaviors learned from exposure to that society.

Could it be that the generations of Ammon and Moab birthed from Lot's daughters, viewed their lives through the lenses of these women's pasts, and their behavioral practices? Further biblical research will show that the behavioral practices of the Moabites caused the nation of Israel to sin against their God, in the book of Numbers Chapter 25. This suggests that certain behaviors have the capacity to become a social norm in certain cultures; and if they come from a place of trauma or a skewed world view, can easily influence other cultures.

The only way to combat the outcome of a culturally embedded behavior pattern, is to give an alternative to the behavior being disposed. To simply do away with behavior that has been determined abnormal will result in resistance or a certain level of defiance. An alternative way must be presented to replace the undesired behavior, otherwise the behavior is presented to the generation, increases in its potential to breed a culture that will continue to repeat the self-validating and self-defeating behavioral patterns of its predecessors. The outcome is that the generation will retain issues, and dilemmas that are remediable- and yet remain unresolved.

Feminist biblical scholar Phyllis Trible's survey of three approaches to the study of women in Scripture says, "certain feminists concentrate upon discovering and recovering traditions that challenge the culture, [and] that task involves highlighting neglected texts."[vii] While the behavior of Lot's daughters is indefensible, they were likely making a decision based on desperation to preserve their lives; the distance (physical, and religious) between themselves and other family members, the recent abandonment of their mother, and rejection from an entire culture that would have rather raped men than marry virgin women. It is difficult to pinpoint where this behavioral pattern began. However, based on the expected age in which women bore children in this culture, it was during the stages of early adolescence.

Womanist theologian Emilie M. Townes wrote, "Exploring evil as a cultural production highlights the systematic construction of truncated narratives designed to support and perpetuate structural inequities and forms of social oppression."[viii] This insight calls for the careful examination of those who are strategic in oppressing the weak, and ensuring their sense of voiceless-ness. There is a voice that supersedes authority in the physical realm and permeates itself beyond the psychological into the core of the spirit. It is the voice of God which is translated to us as the voice of Truth.[ix]

I am going to introduce to you a woman who sat in a broken pew of the average postmodern urban church. My desire is that you – the reader- will be able to draw distinct similarities between her story, the story of Lot's daughters, and possibly many other women in the Bible. Surely, you will notice that the woman in that pew had to struggle with a behavior that had been introduced to her as a child. Although she was powerless and innocent, she was introduced to manipulation, survival, and behavioral norm due to the abandonment of her mother and the tainted religious views of her father.

Unresolved Issues and the Broken Pew

On an average Sunday morning, in an average postmodern church, located in an economically strained urban society, this little girl who is now a woman of color, walks into a church in her neighborhood. She is in her early thirties. She has recently survived an abortion. She had feelings of guilt, shame and resentment. She is emotionally broken and wrestling with various types of psychological trauma from her past. We are not sure what dilemmas she is currently facing. She could be a single mother. She could be a woman who is struggling with her sexual identity. She could be facing poverty, stressed by government institutions and requirements for meeting the qualifications for receiving subsidies. She might be a student, who is trying to better herself through education.

Regardless, even though we are given a glimpse of her background story, we will never know, and she may never be able to articulate the full extent of the issues she faced between the ages of 17 and 30 years old. However, when she walked into the sanctuary of this urban church, anyone who was paying attention to her demeanor could discern that it had been a long time since she had been to church. She was struggling with the spiritual and psychological burden of depression.

Anyone, which was everyone, who was looking

would notice that she had tried to put on some makeup to hide the physical abuse and emotional scars she had suffered over the years. She arrived at the sanctuary of the postmodern urban church, in her neighborhood, with the desire to blend in.

As she walked through the door, with some expectation of relief, the greeter looked at her with smile-less disapproval and pointed her toward a random section in the left side of the sanctuary. The experience she was about to have within this sanctuary, had immediately been hindered by this awkward treatment. Because of it, she was confused. She didn't really know where to sit. So, she sat in an empty pew in the back of the sanctuary, located in a far-off corner, disconnected and alone. No one else greeted her. No one smiled in her direction. Actually no one was smiling at all. It seemed that no one was willing to welcome the new soul who had entered the sanctuary of the average postmodern urban church, in her neighborhood.

Sporadically, people in the congregation turned around to take a glance at the new face. Some looked at her clothes, others at her shoes. One person looked at her, and then turned to whisper something to her neighbor. This woman was already confused about her seat, and now she was uncomfortable. She could feel the secret whispers going around about her in the church. Even if the people weren't talking about her, she felt that they were. The young woman wondered if she was sitting in the wrong seat. She began to wonder if she had on the wrong clothes. She needed something- and she thought she would get it by coming to the church. Although her discomfort increased, she refused to leave. She folded her arms, self-consciously thinking, "I thought church was where people came to feel better." Rather than being invited into the worship experience, she was now watching *"Urban Church"* happen as though she were a spectator, and the performances of the urban church was a live stage play in a theater.

As she watched this production, she suddenly felt she had the most uncomfortable seat in the house. For reasons unknown to her she could not engage the atmosphere. She didn't feel comfortable standing and clapping while the singing was going on. She also didn't know the words to the songs. As the worship continued, she began to feel discouraged. Finally, she sat down in her seat. She began to look around the room from that isolated, disconnected space in the sanctuary of this postmodern urban church, watching the people around her. She shifted her weight to find comfort in her seat, but the seat felt like it was broken. Why couldn't she get comfortable in the place she believed she would find the most comfort? Was it her broken spirit? Was her spirit so heavy that it forced her to sit in that seat? Or was it the broken pew? Is this the place where broken people sit? Or maybe it could it have been something broken in the atmosphere of worship?

.

Chapter One: Understanding Womanist Theology

1.1 A Brief Overview

Womanist theology attempts to help women of color see, affirm, and have confidence in the importance of their worship experience and faith, which are useful for determining the character of the Christian religion in the African American community. It is a religious conceptual framework, which reconsiders and revises traditions, practices, scriptures, and biblical interpretation with a special lens to empower and liberate African-American women in America.[x] The goals of womanist theology include interrogating the social construction of black womanhood in relation to the black community, and assuming a perspective such that African-American women can live emboldened lives within the African-American community, and within the larger society.[xi] Womanist theologian Carolyn Akua L. McCray says:

"A Womanist theological approach is necessary because it recognizes, respects, and affirms the necessity of the personal spiritual experience, in terms of helping Black women in their exploration and enhancement of a proper relationship with intimate and ultimate reality."[xii]

Some of the tasks of womanist theology target excavating the life stories of abused, economically strained, and yet empowered women of African American descent within the Church. The challenges that womanist theology seeks to overcome is the perpetual voiceless-ness of women of color. Womanist theology also attempts to offer a greater understanding of the "languages" of black women.[xiii] Womanist theology is strongly associated with black feminism, but it is not to be confused as being the same.[xiv] Womanist theology is not isolated to women of African descent; it attempts to embrace women of color and their stories all over the world.[xv]

Womanist theology challenges all oppressive forces impeding especially the black women's struggle for survival and for the development of a positive, productive quality of life conducive to women's and the family's freedom and well-being.[xvi] Womanist theology opposes all oppression based on race, sex, class, sexual preference, physical ability, and caste.[xvii]

Alice Walker defines a womanist as a feminist of color who is willful, serious, loving, and "committed to survival and wholeness of entire people, male and female."[xviii] One of the main reasons womanist theological perspectives are essential to incorporate in the worship experience of the postmodern Christian churches of this era is because Christian womanist methodology includes four essential elements to community building.[xix]

1.2 The Elements of Womanist Theology

The first of the elements is that womanist theology is multi-dialogical, meaning that the dialogue focuses in on the well-being of the people regardless of age, race, sexual preference, and gender.[xx] The focuses of womanist theological views are on freedom from societal, political, and religious oppression. The second womanist element is the liturgical approach, which carries over from secular social concerns to the social concerns in the predominantly black church community. Third, the didactic element of womanist methodology incorporates the moral wisdom and moral heritage of black oppressed and abused women, offering a theological perspective on moral ethics and insights about moral life, also supporting justice, survival, and a productive life for poverty-stricken women, men, and children.[xxi]

Lastly, the teaching and womanist theological language uses stories, images, and metaphors to incorporate the oppressive history, culture, and religious experience (of the black women), into the Christians community to help shape the Church society. To use this theological approach is to address and define the response of the church toward mental health transformation, views on oppression, and redemptive suffering.

Womanist theology is similar to and derived from Liberation theology.[xxii] It is important to know that womanists share in the belief that *education is liberation.*

True womanists tend to encourage others to become empowered with the goal of survival for the community by being educated, and by reaching a level of self-awareness. In addition, womanists also believe that building community and maintaining healthy relationships are key factors pertaining to the survival and affirmation of self-worth for the community and the individuals living in it.

1.3 Strategic Methods of Womanist Theology

While the strategic methods of womanist theology are claimed by 'black women,' they are not limited to women solely because of the woman's gender. Its aim is in the direction of liberation and empowerment for both genders. Its response methods to psychological and spiritual disorientation due to traumatic experiences are not limited by gender specificity, as in feminist theology. To womanists, men, especially men of color are essential to the building and empowerment of the black community. Men are not, however, the central focus of womanist theology (as in black theology). Emotional, spiritual, and psychological healing, reconciliation, relationship, and restoration have equal importance in Womanist theology.[xxiii]

1.4 Womanist Preaching and Post Modernity

According to William H. Willimon, author of *The Intrusive Word*: *Preaching to the Unbaptized*, "modernity refers to someone who thinks that he or she is answerable to no story other than the one he or she has personally chosen."[xxiv] Theologian Thomas Oden stated, "Whatever outlasts modernity is postmodern."[xxv] Postmodernism is a cultural development which started in the late twentieth century, characterized by a rejection of absolutes and objective definitions of reality.[xxvi] How can a person define reality without acknowledgement of absolutes? Absolutes and objectivity exist in reality. He affirms the thought that a person, who dismisses the absolutes, rationality, and objectivity of life, yet still trying to define his or her life, has created a formula for insanity. Womanist preachers often deal in absolutes when preaching from the pulpit and in conversation, since many of us hold to absolutes based on our life experiences.

As I began to reflect on our woman who is now sitting in a broken pew… I wondered, where was the womanist theology in the atmosphere of worship? I asked myself, how could I better understand the reason the pew felt so broken, unbalanced and uncomfortable. How could this pew be fixed? How could the atmosphere be changed? Could it be that the discomfort of the seat was more comfortable than the atmosphere?

Chapter Two:
The Broken Pew

2.1 The Broken Pew Overview

This chapter will give a brief overview of the importance of womanist theology as it applies to the worship experience for women, presented as a regime of mediation (chapter five). Here, I make the claim that Womanist responses are effective in administering treatment for and a responsive remedy to TbPSD.[xxvii] As a reminder, just in case it was not mentioned in the beginning of this research, TbPSD is an acronym for Trauma-based Psychological and Spiritual Disorientation. This chapter will introduce a case study of a woman sitting I the average postmodern urban congregation, disoriented by not only TbPSD, but at the base of the condition is its source, Domestic Violence (DV). Domestic Violence includes physical, psychological and spiritual traumatization, which is often dismissed within the societies who accept the behavior as normal to its culture. This chapter should be approached keeping in mind that the effects of Trauma-based Psycho-Spiritual Disorientation has silenced many voices within the postmodern urban church, due to the fact that it is so easily dismissed or passed off as a form of mental illness. People will use phrases such as; "She's crazy," or "She's just looking for attention." These types of phrases often silence those who are suffering with the condition even more.

In this chapter as well as throughout this work, I define the postmodern church in the economically strained social construct as the "urban church." This urban church is identified for the purpose of this work, in contrast to suburban and rural churches. This is not to claim that the rural and urban churches have a different set of issues or problems; nor does it suggest that the urban church is the only church isolated in a broken atmosphere. Yet, this work targets at improving the response of the urban church toward the matters of spiritual and psychological trauma for women of color.

2.2 The Broken Spirit

I want to direct your attention to a chapter in Genesis 34. Jacob the son of Isaac, son of Abraham, has a daughter named Dinah. Shechem the Hivite raped her. Shechem was a man who had a certain level of power and control within his society and country. The issue for me with this story is the way Dinah was treated by her own society after this trauma happened and was disclosed. First, Shechem only wanted to marry Dinah only after he had violated her by making a deal with Jacob, possibly to escape the consequences of his action against this young woman. Does this behavior suggest that violation is excused, allowed, and accepted through the father and siblings after disclosure, without regard for the feelings and trauma place on the victim? Next, was a false sense of accountability on the part of both the violator and those who had the responsibility to protect the innocence of the young woman. Dinah's immediate social structure seemingly refused to acknowledge her feelings. Of course, there is an acknowledgement that she has been raped. It is public knowledge based on the way that her brothers respond to this violation. The response of Dinah's brothers obviously shows their outrage, and their anger toward this disrespect committed against them. It seems that their taking this violation so personal became centralized on their own revenge rather than on the feelings of their sister, and the women of their community. As the story goes on, Shechem and his father ended up making a deal with Jacob and Dinah's brothers, determining how Dinah was going to live out the rest of her life.

The text does not include whether anyone asked Dinah how she felt, or how she would choose to live her life. Her brothers ended up killing Shechem and all of his people later in the text. However, this act can be interpreted as retaliation for Shechem's disrespect personally against the men of the community rather than their sister. Did anyone consider Dinah's feelings? Was she pregnant from this traumatic experience? We never find out what happened to Dinah, because her voice is lost and overpowered by the narrative of those in the society who have more power than her. If she had become pregnant from the rape, what happened to the child? Why does she, and her voice disappear from the narrative? The focus shifts to the brother's and their acts of redemptive violence against the Hivites, but does it restore the voice of Dinah? Did she have to submit to the decision and live out the rest of her days without a voice or restitution?

Feminist theologian Phyllis Trible states "although not every story involving female and male [relationships] is so terrifying, the narrative literature nevertheless makes clear that from birth to death the Hebrew woman belonged to men."[xxviii] Trible's research confirms that historical biblical texts define women as property of men. Was the retaliation of Dinah's brothers against Shechem and the Hivites about Dinah, or merely because they did not ask first, thus taking property that did not belong to them? This is a statement intensifies an unresolved issue for women who have been abused and are currently suffering with Trauma-based Psycho-Spiritual Disorientation (TbPSD).

In response to Dinah and for many women who have lived through the trauma of Domestic Violence, which includes adult rape and Child Sexual Abuse, and are sitting in the broken pews of the postmodern urban church; our stories are relived and revived when we look at new and current situations through the lenses of our pasts. I wonder, how many abusive men have initiated violence against other abusive men, simply because the situation concerning woman in question was viewed as a violation of property rather than an act of defense for a violation of rights. Mandy Evans states, "We often view new events through the same system that took us in that direction in the first place. The new events then validate our conclusions from the past, because that is how we see things."[xxix] By doing this, the woman risks repeating the same behavioral patterns of her past, and as a result re-validates and re-affirm her doubts, fears, and the fate of unfavorable outcomes. I wonder, if we apply what Evan's statement to Dinah's story, could this be the reason that some women have a psychologically embedded mistrust for men within their own social contexts?

The habitual and psychological process of women who have been sexually traumatized, reliving, revisiting, and revalidating the past, become psychological and theological tools which shape and mold one's personalities, identities, and roles pertaining to our social location within our communities. The repeated violations women face from their immediate societies have a direct effect on their responses to the atmosphere in which they live.

This pattern of behavior developed from reliving traumatic experiences repeatedly is often imbalanced, because it is not isolated to a physical or psychological nature. The pattern of behavior involves the spirit of the woman, which in my own opinion is linked to the limbic system and functions of the hippocampus. The spiritual and psychological needs of women and the responses from the churches they attend, are often polarized as it pertains to situations that have the potential to re-injure their mind, body, and spirit. It is not only the mind body and spirit of the woman which is at risk, but the mind body and spirit of the entire church and everyone sitting in the broken pews.

2.3 Broken: Polarization and Pluralistic Ignorance

Words such as "devastation, destruction and disorder" depict images related to divided families, broken communication within societies and classes of people, in conjunction with perpetual cultural dilemmas. In his chapter on "The Social Context," Psychologist, Benjamin B. Lahey explains polarization, He states:

"Whenever groups of persons discuss dilemmas, they are much more likely to take extreme positions and recommend risky options. The discussion of the issues in groups often leads to the polarization of thinking by pushing [ones] opinions toward one extreme "pole" of the issue."[xxx]

The same extreme behavior applies to the individual as it does in the social context of a church. What happens when the trauma of devastation divides one body, one thought, or an element into two? Please keep in mind here that we are not isolating this divide to the individual woman, but to the congregation which is the social context in which the woman is a part of.

Can this term polarization refer to the spiritual and psychological destruction wrought on a person victimized by forms of domestic violence such as Childhood Sexual Abuse? By definition *polarization* is defined as tendency for a group discussion to make beliefs and attitudes more extreme.[xxxi] If this is the case, what happens when a woman who suffers from Trauma-based Psycho-Spiritual Disorientation (TbPSD) walks into the social context of a postmodern urban church and directed to a random broken pew? We will discuss more about TbPSD and what it means in the next chapter. However, how can we interpret the feelings of a person, regardless of their gender, who looks for a place to help them articulate their concerns and are made to feel as if they are in a place saturated with condemnation, ridicule, and/or prejudice.

When this (or any) traumatized woman, as described earlier, enters the sanctuary of the average postmodern urban church, and is pointed in the direction toward a random pew, it reveals a diffusion of responsibility in the church's response to such a dilemma. Michelle Alexander in her book *"The New Jim Crow: Mass Incarceration in the Age of Colorblindness."* describes this phenomenon as *Pluralistic Ignorance.* She states, "Many people struggling to cope with the stigma of imprisonment have no idea that their neighbors are struggling with the same grief, shame, and isolation."[xxxii] Where Alexander uses the term imprisonment, I would like to use the term psychological bondage. Replacing the term foreshadows the emphasis on Trauma-based Psycho-Spiritual Disorientation. The reason, for the change in the term is because disorientation connotes a temporary rather than permanent condition. If we couple this Alexander's phenomenon with the definition of polarization, we reveal the two extremes of the average postmodern urban church. Below are two definitions.

1) **The Ecclesial Church**, for the purpose of this work, identifies itself as an under-equipped culture of urban populated churches with minimal education attempting to remedy a psychological behavior. It has a weak sense of spirituality saturated by dogmatism, and a lack of the tangible resources required to respond effectively.

2) **The Institutional Church** has plenty of resources: financial, social, and political, but little understanding or compassion for the spiritual condition of the person. This church lacks the cultural components of spirituality, witnessing, and evangelism.

While both are effective in working on specific parts of the overall dilemma a woman is facing when she walks through the doors of the postmodern urban church. However, when it comes to dealing with spiritual and psychological trauma, polarization, and pluralistic ignorance- the Ecclesial Church and the Christian Institutional Church work on opposite end of the pole, thus preventing synergy from what I call balancing the books.

The church must not only consider the polarization of the women [and men in some cases] sitting in their pews, but it must also consider its ignorance of the situations facing its parishioners, and the polarization of itself as what we consider the "Body of Christ". While both responses from both the Ecclesial and Institutional church are effective, when used individually, the reality is that only one extreme is satisfied at a time.

For the church to respond effectively to spiritual and psychological trauma, it is necessary to create a consubstantial approach to a consubstantial dilemma.[xxxiii] It is unfair not to note that the typical postmodern urban church society has tried to respond to traumatic issues with topical dogmatism and ritualistic practices, often masked as remedies. When we identify the postmodern urban church only as only an ecclesial body, in comparison to professional mental health institutions, it suggests that there is a weakened consensus in understanding as it pertains to Trauma-based Psycho-Spiritual Disorientation.

Isolating the church as a simple ecclesial body shifts the responsibility of dealing with psychological trauma to secularized institutions, such as mental health centers and family crisis hotlines. Mental health institutions, as it compares to the postmodern urban church, are often considered to only have the ability to respond with remedies such as medications that control and manage the symptoms of psychological trauma, while missing the spiritual relevance, and misdiagnosing, misnaming the spiritual cause of the behaviors displayed by the person dealing with the trauma.

2.4 The Name Game

The ability to name the spiritual and psychological condition is an important element of the process of treating the condition. Naming is an imperative for both the church and the women who sit in the broken pews because it assigns identity to the issues affecting the identity of the individual. The *DSM*, which is short for *Diagnostic and Statistical Manual of Mental Disorders* is a tool used for naming the psychological results of people suffering from the effects of psychological trauma. I would consider the DSM a useful tool, because it offers explanation for some of the names used in the institutions responsible for responding to persons dealing with psychological trauma. One of the goals of this study is to introduce a name or a term that I was not able to find in the DSM that might help us to understand the post effects of traumatic life situations in consideration of both psychological and spiritual well-being. Rather than isolating the name to only deal with psychological ailments, I feel that women need a name that is inclusive of their spiritual oppression as well: *Trauma-Based Psycho-Spiritual Disorientation.*

To explain, *disorientation* carries a different definition than words such as devastation, destruction, and disorder. According to psychologist Pam Nugent M.S., disorientation is the impaired ability to identify oneself in relation to time, place, and other aspects of surroundings.[xxxiv] In his book, *The Message of the Psalms,* Walter Brueggemann stated, "Life is also savagely marked by disequilibrium, incoherence, and unrelieved asymmetry."[xxxv] Brueggemann's phrase points to the obvious; that there are situations in life that happen to each and every one of us, some of those "things," whatever we choose to define them as, disorient us. The Psycho-Spiritual aspect of the term 'disorientation,' refers to both the psychological and spiritual location of the individual. How disoriented a person is will also determine how displaced he or she is as it pertains to his or her social identity/ location. Since we have established that "trauma" affects both the spiritual and psychological location of an individual, Psycho-Spiritual Disorientation (a misappropriation of self-identity) is the result.

It brings to our awareness that women who sit in the sanctuaries of our churches in discomfort, longing for relief from the burden of using tools that are no longer useful in their lives; must reach the conclusion that the burdens of spiritual and psychological bondage (as in Alexander's example) come from and are based on a deeply embedded psychological malfunction in their beliefs. Women dealing with TbPSD caused by Childhood Sexual Abuse have a skewed social location, due to a misinformed identity about themselves, and disoriented cognitive reasoning. The result is "Trauma-based Psycho- Spiritual Disorientation."

Social location, cognitive reasoning, and a sense of identity are all important components to shaping the world view of an individual. It is equally important to understand how memory plays a significant role in identifying a person's social location as he or she progresses through life. Later, in this work I will discuss more about the stages of life based on Eric Erikson's Theory of Adult Development. It is important to briefly mention the theory here because we are about to discuss how traumatic experiences create dilemmas, and how we deal with the situations create memories, which shapes the world view of the individual.

2.4 Memories, Hippocampus, & Hormones

Is it possible, that the reason the postmodern urban church is not responding effectively to those individuals similar to the woman sitting in the rear of the church because most churches, when it comes to women, do not consider Childhood Sexual Abuse to be a form of domestic violence? Domestic violence is a sensitive subject for many individuals who have experienced it. Often reliving the traumatic experience of the past can conjure mixed emotions, create identity confusion, and

Trauma-based Psycho-Spiritual Disorientation. The hippocampus of the brain is responsible for retaining memories throughout the life of an individual. So, what kind of an effect does memories of Childhood Sexual Abuse, Domestic Violence have on the woman sitting in the broken pew in the rear of the postmodern urban church?

The hippocampus is a small organ within the brain's temporal lobe. It is an important part of the limbic system which is the region that regulates emotions."[xxxvi] When this part of the brain experiences excessive trauma, it inhibits behavioral responses previously learnt by the individual. Thus far, in our Biblical references, both Lots daughters (Genesis Chapter 16) and any women connected to Dinah's story (Genesis 34) may have developed a way of coping with the trauma they experienced and passed those methods, and behaviors in response to the trauma to the generations that followed. The limbic system, which regulates emotions, is responsible for transferring information into memory.[xxxvii] Most people remember things based on how it made them feel. As for many women who enter the sanctuaries of the postmodern urban church, what do we think they feel when they have been traumatized not only at home, but re-traumatized when they are treated poorly at the place where they seek comfort?

According to the research by *Harvard Medical Health*, "several genes influence the stress response, leaving us more or less likely to become depressed in response to trouble."[xxxviii] Keeping in mind that Traumatic experiences such as Childhood Sexual Abuse, and any form of Domestic Violence translates for the purpose of this discussion as "trouble." In addition, the experts at Harvard explain that depression is also genetic. The article states:

> "It is well known that depression and bipolar disorder run in families. The strongest evidence for this comes from the research on bipolar disorder. Half of those with bipolar disorder have a relative with a similar pattern of mood fluctuations."[xxxix]

Once again, we have revisited a term that has to do with *polarization*, and its relationship to trauma. Now, we have also included the factors related to family genetics as it relates to the response behaviors by women [or men] in response to psychological trauma. The research directs this conversation to the idea that the learned behaviors that many women experience are genetically psychological, meaning that the response patterns are inherited from the previous generation's genes. In my opinion, since this is proven true, a more serious dilemma is created for the woman sitting in the broken pew of the postmodern church. *When she says to herself, "I thought church was the place people came to feel better,"* it suggests that there was a belief in the previous generation, that the church was a place of solace. As a side note to this notion, when I reflect on the behavior of the descendants of Lot's Daughters, it gave me a different outlook on their behavior as a nation. Based on the research, the behaviors we often see in the biblical texts, are genetically passed from generation to generation.

The Hippocampus' essential function is to create new memories, without it, many of us would be stuck in the pasts of our lives, re-living whatever experiences exist there. If the new memory for the woman directed to a random pew in the postmodern church sanctuary, is one of mistreatment, judgment, gossip, etc.; what will be the behavioral response she will pass on to the generation following her? Could this be why our pews are in decline?

For those who have had ideal peace filled childhoods, limited amounts of traumatic experiences, and instances and memories of love and acceptance-especially within the social contexts of "church," experiencing instances of nostalgia are blissful and not as pain-filled as someone who suffered from psychological and spiritual oppression, dur to Childhood Sexual Abuse and Domestic Violence. Medical evidence shows that the hippocampus reduces in size in people who have severe depression and other forms of mental illness.[xl] This is interpreted with the understanding that the amount of trauma the hippocampus endures the more likely it is to shrink in size. The Hippocampus is linked to estrogen levels in the body, which is especially important in the discussion as it pertains to women.[xli] The increase in estrogen increases the synaptic density, which means that there is an increase in connections to other nerve cells.[xlii] However, when someone is suffering with severe depression or unable to create new memories due to damage to the hippocampus or a reduction in the synaptic connections, a variety mood disorders and behavioral dysfunction result.

Later in this study, you will find a pyramid model displaying *Maslow's Hierarchy of Needs* theory. I plan to compare the model of *Hormone and Mood Disorders* presented by John Phelps, to Maslow's Hierarchy of Needs. The correlation shown is as one moves up Phelps' scale, the needs presented by Maslow are less physiological, and more psychological. Could it be that every mood disorder presented by Phelps requires a correlated response from Maslow's hierarchy of needs? Is it possible that women who suffer with psychological and/or neurological damage to the hippocampus due to traumatic experiences, which are coupled with a decrease in estrogen levels or other hormonal /chemical imbalances – are suffering from multi-levels of Trauma – based Psycho-Spiritual Disorientation? My theory is that Phelps' Model of Hormones and Mood Disorders shows that if correlated properly, prove that treatments which lead to a cure are available to women who are suffering with the condition.

When the cause of Trauma-based Psycho-

Spiritual Disorientation is understood, as well as treatment administered effectively, a holistic approach to the dilemma becomes available to women silently suffering with it. The purpose of the pyramid in fig. 1 is not to be used to make a diagnosis for Bipolar II. I use this model of hormones and mood disorders helps us to understand the type or likened behavior displayed by women during the influx of hormones (which are influenced by the limbic system), and for the purpose of this research, the probability of resulting behavior when psychological and spiritual needs are not being met.

A Working Model of Hormones and Mood Disorders

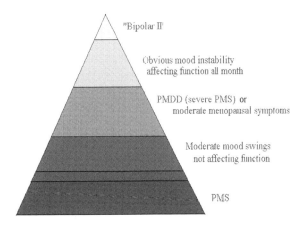

* Figure 1- *A Working Model of Hormones and Mood Disorders,"*
  James Phelps MD. Psycheducation.org/hormones and mood disorders.

Throughout the years, psychologists and medical experts have diagnosed many women oppressed by spiritual and psychological trauma by giving names and titles to their behavior to treat their physiological needs. A biblical reference is linked to the story of the hemorrhaging woman in Mark chapter five.[xliii] Yet, have these mental and medical institution and prescription drugs only offered a false remedy to the manifestations of a spiritual and psychological dilemma? Do the treatments ever deal with the source or the cause of their diagnostic findings?

In the next Chapter, we will look at the statistical data in hope to answer the question: how many broken pews are in the postmodern urban church?

Chapter Three:
The Broken Pews &
Broken People

3.1 Statistical data

The pews in the postmodern urban church are broken when there is a refusal to acknowledge the spiritual and psychological condition of the person sitting in them. I have personified the pews, because I feel there is a need to bridge this conversation to the personification of the church. The pews, whether they are broken or not, are more than just furniture in the sanctuary of the church. However, if the church is simply another representation of an institution and the sanctuary is typified as just another room for a business or social meeting, then the pews are as dead as the institutional church.

Statistical data shows that there are on average over 42 million survivors who have disclosed victimization by Childhood Sexual Abuse. Yet, many have never disclosed that they were ever abused. With the ratios provided through research, there are victims of Childhood Sexual Abuse (which is a form of Domestic Violence), sitting in the comfortably padded pews of our postmodern urban churches. They sit there in discomfort, silenced, voiceless, and spiritually and psychologically broken. It is my hope that this chapter will illustrate how these statistics apply to the average post-modern church sanctuary when a woman walks in and is pointed to a random pew on any random Sunday.

According to the National Center for Victims of Crime, the prevalence of Childhood Sexual Abuse is seldom reported which makes it difficult to determine.[xliv] Experts agree that the unreported incidences are far greater than incidences reported to authorities. Statistics below represent some of the research done on child sexual abuse.[xlv] The U.S. Department of Health and Human Services Children's Bureau report "Child Maltreatment 2010" found that 9.2% of victimized children were sexually assaulted. Studies by David Finkelhor, Director of the Crimes against Children Research Center, show that:

- 1 in 5 girls and 1 in 20 boys is a victim of child sexual abuse;
- Self-report studies show that 20% of adult females and 5-10% of adult males recall a childhood sexual assault or sexual abuse incident;
- During a one-year period in the U.S., 16% of youth ages 14 to 17 had been sexually victimized;
- Over the course of their lifetime, 28% of U.S. youth ages 14 to 17 had been sexually victimized;
- Children are most vulnerable to Childhood Sexual Abuse between the ages of 7 and 13.

Using the comparison of broken pews to represent broken people, in a church, which seats 100 people, 25 of the pews show signs that they are psychologically and spiritually broken in this way. These statistics to say nothing of other forms of abuse people suffer which are not sexual. Twenty of the pews belong to women who are willing to voice their lament and cry out for help and healing. However, how many times has the postmodern urban church denied women who would voice their lament in the sanctuary the opportunity to do so? Proverbs 25:20 says, "Like one who takes away a garment on a cold day, or like vinegar poured on a wound, is one who sings songs to a heavy heart" (NIV). Returning to Brueggemann's conversation on disorientation he stated, "I think that serious religious use of the lament psalms has been minimal because we have believed that faith does not mean to acknowledge and embrace negativity."[xlvi] However, in the postmodern society the focus has been on one that only sings "happy songs." How offensive, in the midst of suffering, the people, especially women, who have never disclosed the abuse they have suffered, sit in silence, and denied the psychological and spiritual remedy of naming their sorrow or participating in a communal lament?

3.2 Identifying Needs

Consider Maslow's theory of hierarchy of needs/growth development when he implies that when a need is unfulfilled in one place, people will go to another place where they believe their needs will be satisfied. Humanistic psychologist Carl Rogers (1902-1987) agrees with Maslow's theory but adds that for a person to grow they need an environment that provides them with genuineness, acceptance, and empathy.[xlvii] If an individual's environment does not provide them these basic elements they need for growth and development, such as in the postmodern urban church, they will turn to other outlets readily offered to them. We will not dismiss that there are plenty of unhealthy outlets for women to turn to such as drugs, alcohol, promiscuity, etc. Some of the more positive outlets offered to women are in the form of private practice therapy sessions, crisis response centers, and psychiatric hospitals, which are what we would consider 'good' institutions, but also have another purpose; to generate revenue for the mental health care industry.

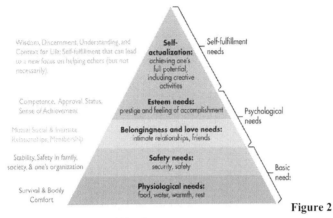

Figure 2

Maslow's Hierarchy of Needs:
https://www.templatemonster.com/blog/maslow-hierarchy-of-needs-content-creation. (accessed 1/13/2018)

Treating the after effects of Childhood Sexual Abuse holds a significant role in the mental health care industry, and yet still poses a serious healthcare crisis.[xlviii] Statistics show that the direct cost of mental health care tops 97 billion dollars per year, and indirect mental health costs average 110 billion dollars annually.[xlix] Ten percent of the 200 billion dollars of mental health costs per year is attributed to child sexual abuse survivors.[l] Treating victims of Childhood Sexual Abuse impacts the medical health care industry because of its relation to sexual behavioral practices of its survivors who have not received proper mental or medical treatment.

According to a statistical report provided by *Darkness to Light Child Abuse Prevention* agency, "healthcare expenses are one of the most critical issues facing Americans today."[li] In an adult retrospective study by Finklehor, 27 percent of the women and 16 percent of the men interviewed, reported victimization from Childhood Sexual Abuse. The median age for the occurrence of reported abuse was 9 years old for both male and female. Sexual victimization prior to age 8 was 22 percent for boys, and 23 percent for girls.[lii] From the study, 42 percent of the women and 33 percent of the men reported never having disclosed the abuse to anyone.[liii] In addition, individuals who have undergone this type of traumatic experience reported having a sense of lack in their lives. This includes, but is not limited to low self-esteem, low self-image, and lack of self-respect for one's own body.[liv]

Research expert, Larry K. Brown cites data that shows adolescents with a history of sexual abuse are significantly more likely than those who have not, to engage in sexual behavior that puts them at risk for HIV infection.[lv] Could this be because they have a need to feel loved, so much so that they engage in risky sexual practices to fulfill a need for love and belonging? They are three times more likely to have lower impulse control and inconsistent condom use, which result in a higher rate of sexually transmitted diseases and unplanned pregnancy.[lvi] Teenage pregnancy and sexually transmitted disease in the United States is responsible for 17.4 billion dollars of overall healthcare costs. Of that 17.4 billion about 3.5 billion is attributed to Child Sexual Abuse survivors.[lvii]

Due to the poor economic condition of the survivors, most of the counseling these individuals receive will not address their current sexual behavior or deal with the underlying issues. According to Maslow every person needs to achieve levels of esteem and self-actualization which are beyond simple physiological needs. In order to accomplish this task, the individual must begin to move past the psychological needs to the satisfy the needs for self-fulfillment. When the psychological and self-fulfillment needs of the individual are not met within the medical institutions society provides, the result for adolescent survivors of Child Sexual Abuse is that they will continue to re-experience anxiety and trauma for years (possibly into their adult stages).[lviii] As previously stated the individual (adolescent or adult) will often turn to some other method of coping to attempt to satisfy their needs. Again, these methods of coping with Trauma-based Psycho-Spiritual Disorientation have potential to become genetic behavioral responses that are passed from generation to generation.

Abortion clinics provide a quick and detrimental solution to the issue of unplanned pregnancy. However, these quick, impulsive solutions are merely physiological, because they remedy the unplanned pregnancy, by terminating it. Unfortunately, the behavior that caused the pregnancy is not effectively addressed. Abortion methods used as an immediate remedy leaves sexually abused, poverty-stricken women who live in urban societies with severe emotional scars. Often due to fear of the opinions of the congregants of the postmodern urban church, many women sit in silence, on broken pews, in broken atmospheres.

Each year, broad cross sections of U.S. women obtain abortions. As of 2014, some 60% of women having abortions were in their 20s; 59% had one or more children; 86% were unmarried; 75% were economically disadvantaged; and 62% reported a religious affiliation.[lix] No racial or ethnic group made up a majority: Some 39% of women obtaining abortions were white, 28% were black, 25% were Hispanic and 9% were of other racial or ethnic backgrounds.[lx] What does this say about the needs of women? While this statistic shows that white women were the majority to have abortions in 2014, at 39%, Women of color in general which include Black/ African American, Hispanic and "Other," account for 62%. How many of these women of color, due to their economic and social status had access to affordable care for their psychological and spiritual needs? Did many of them turn to drugs and other forms of substance abuse to cope with the psychological and spiritual illnesses?

Other statistical studies show that adolescents forced to have sex, meaning that they have been sexually abused, are three times more likely to develop psychiatric disorders, and/or abuse alcohol and drugs in adulthood.[lxi] Drug use is likely because the person is making an attempt to reconcile a psychiatric need with tools that are not only useless, but destructive. I personally believe that drug use is a method that people use to relieve the asymmetry trauma caused in their lives. There is a clinical assumption that children, who feel compelled to keep sexual abuse a secret, suffer a greater psychiatric distress than victims who disclose the secret and receive support.[lxii] Without support, depression effects the hippocampus and the behavioral responses of the individual. This proves that those traumatically abused, especially in cases of Child Sexual Abuse, are most likely to develop and establish a cycle of violence and abusive behavior in their own homes and communities.[lxiii] This cycle includes but is not limited to:

- Domestic violence -physical, spousal, relationship abuse;
- Sexual Abuse-rape, incest, molestation, sexual identity crisis, abortion;
- Societal/Spiritual Abuse- cultic behavior, manipulation, abuse of power;
- Substance Abuse, which includes use of controlled substances, antidepressants, and abuse of prescription drugs.

In 2013, the Affordable Care Act approved by President Obama expanded insurance coverage to 62 million Americans, including those with mental health and substance use disorders.[lxiv] Before the expansion, insurance agencies and patients were limited by what services qualified for coverage and many Americans were denied healthcare coverage to treat mental illness and substance use disorders.[lxv]

> "While almost all large group plans and most small group plans include coverage for some mental health and substance use disorder services, there are gaps in coverage and many people with some coverage of these services do not currently receive the benefit of federal parity protections. The final rule implementing the Essential Health Benefits directs non-grandfathered health plans in the individual and small group markets to cover mental health, and substance abuse services as well as to comply with the federal parity law requirements beginning in 2014."[lxvi]

Could this have been an attempt by the institutional agencies and the economic powers of the government, to try to help those, especially women gain access to effective methods of care? What then would be the outcome? Would self-actualization come from these institutions designed to assess the psychological condition of the women and men who walk through their doors, or would they leave with a cheap substitute masked as a diagnosis and a prescription that only temporarily resolves a physiological chemical imbalance, while derailing other hormones operating in the body? Will these women of color leave these agencies designed to collect statistical data with diagnosis' they cannot define? These women are subject to being considered abnormal or having an incurable disorder, due to an unfulfilled psychological need caused by the trauma of Childhood Sexual Abuse and domestic violence, is that fair? Have their needs been exploited, for economic gain?

3.3 Abnormal Behavior & Psychological Disorders

Abnormal behavior is a subjective judgment. Abnormality is determined based on the individual's behavioral pattern and his or her potential harm others, and if that harm will cause permanent damage.[lxvii] Depending on one's cultural, religious, and ethical background, the definition of "abnormality" will differ.[lxviii]

As stated earlier, prolonged exposure to stress contributes to mood and behavioral imbalances. Some disorders are purely caused by biological disorders such as brain injury, others are caused by a purely psychological origin such as acute grief, sudden death, or other traumatic occurrences.[lxix] All of these disorders are stress related in a physical or emotional way, due to the link with the limbic system and hippocampus. There are six major classifications of abnormal behavior. The four most common conditions for this discussion on abuse are: Anxiety, Dissociative, Mood, and Personality disorders.[lxx] The previous chapter introduced mood and hormonal disorders but limited them to bipolar disorder due to hormonal imbalances especially in women.

Randy J. Nelson PhD, conducted a study called *Behavioral Endocrinology* which is based on the bidirectional interaction of hormones and behavior.[lxxi] He states in his work that hormones can influence behavior and at the same time behavior can influence hormones.[lxxii] Three prominent hormones that influence behavior are Cortisol, Estradiol, and Testosterone. Cortisol mediates stress responses.[lxxiii] According to an education resource from the society of endocrinology, and for the specific purpose of this dissertation, cortisol also influences memory formation (hippocampus or limbic system). The overproduction of cortisol and exposure to it throughout the body results in mood swings which show in anxiety, depression, or irritability.[lxxiv] Based on this information we can determine that adolescents exposed to excessive amounts of stress due to Childhood Sexual Abuse and Domestic Violence have a higher risk of developing behavioral disorders.

3.4 Behavioral Disorders

One of the major behavioral disorders is anxiety disorder. Anxiety disorders are triggered by a prolonged threat to the individual. These are uneasy senses of general tension and apprehension that make an individual highly uncomfortable and are more common to women than men.[lxxv] Anxiety disorders include phobias, Post-Traumatic Stress Disorder (PTSD), Panic Anxiety (panic attacks), and Obsessive–Compulsive Disorder. One of the most common anxiety disorders in relation to Childhood Sexual Abuse and domestic violence is the post-traumatic stress disorder.

- **Post-Traumatic Stress Disorder** is "the condition caused by extremely stressful experiences in which the person later experiences anxiety and irritability; has upsetting memories, dreams and realistic flashbacks of the experience, and tries to avoid anything that reminds him or her of the experience."[lxxvi] Not all people recover from PTSD and for some the condition can become chronic.

- **Panic and Anxiety** is identified when long periods of calm are broken by an intense uncomfortable attack of anxiety. Obsessive compulsive disorders are caused by anxiety provoking thoughts that will not go away and the irresistible urge to engage in behaviors that are irrational.[lxxvii] Some of these behaviors include recurring fears which cause extreme anxiety, such as losing control and killing someone or of having an incestuous sexual relationship.

- **Dissociative Disorder** is psychologically caused behavior which includes Amnesia, Identity disorder, and depersonalization. It often follows an episode of intense stress, where the person loses most or all recollection of the stressful experience. Dissociative Identity Disorder (formerly known as multiple personality disorder) is a disorder where the individual shifts abruptly from one personality to another. The individual's original personality is conventional, moral, and unhappy, and the alternative personality is the exact opposite. Some mental health experts believe that dissociative identity disorder is the result of physical or sexual abuse during childhood.

- **Oppositional Defiant Disorder,** formerly known as antisocial disorder, which in childhood is displayed as the bullying child who fights, lies, steals, and is often absent from school. As the adult personality develops into an emotionless, guiltless, remorseless individual. They are often violent, and excitement driven. They often become addicted to street drugs and alcohol leaving others victimized by their crimes, violent outbursts, and broken intimacy.[lxxviii] While this disorder is trauma related, it is not directly correlated to Childhood Sexual Abuse.

These are only some of the names disguised as diagnosis given to women [and men] who have suffered trauma in their adolescent years. However, wouldn't giving these terms and names without explanation or definition create more confusion and ambiguity to the individual suffering with the condition? In my opinion, offering a 'name' or diagnosis without definition is metaphorically offering a tool to someone who is not informed as to what to do with it or how to use it. Yet, they must carry the diagnosis with them without understanding its purpose or importance. It becomes a burden, a false attempt at balancing the heaviness of trauma. Regardless of its intent, to name the condition without a definition is not useful to the purpose the woman finding her identity. Once again, we find ourselves being given tools that are useless. By this I mean, what good is naming a condition- without understanding how it works? I believe it is important to know the characteristics of a named condition so that we can respond to its effects with a remedy.

3.5 Abuse affects Identity
      There are various psychological and physical disorders in individuals who have been victimized and

traumatized by sexual abuse.[lxxix] The type of trauma experienced throughout the victim's lifetime and his or her response to the dilemma, will determine the way the person identifies themselves. This concept points to and validates the importance of the hippocampus, memories and mood disorders, and its connection to the behavioral genetics that are passed to the next generation. Those genetic behaviors of Trauma-based Psycho-Spiritual Disorientation, which are passed genetically, begin to shape a culture, a community, and a social response within the postmodern urban church and the neighborhoods they serve.

Erikson's Theory of Identity Development proposes that "psychosocial development continues over the entire lifespan [of an individual] resulting from the interaction among inner instincts and drives with outer cultural and social demands."[lxxx] He also states that in order for a person to progressively develop a stable identity, he or she must "successfully resolve eight crises or dilemmas over the course of a lifetime."[lxxxi] From each stage there is a pair of opposing outcomes to be gained, a virtue or a dilemma.[lxxxii] Each stage presents a need that must be fulfilled. Later in this book, I will compare Maslow's theory to Erickson's. Below is a chart based on Erickson's Adult Development Theory, explaining the stages and fulfilment needs at each stage.

Figure 3: For the purpose of this research, and the language being used, the table has been modified to express that if the needs presented are fulfilled, the result is a virtue. If the needs are not fulfilled, the result is a dilemma.

Stage of Life & Age	Development Needs	Unfulfilled = Dilemma	Fulfilled= Virtue
Stage: 1- Infancy **Ages: Birth – 18 months**	Trust	Mistrust	Hope
Stage: 2- Early Childhood **Ages: 18 months – 2 years**	Autonomy	Shame & Doubt	Will
Stage: 3- Play Age **Ages: 3- 5 years**	Initiative	Guilt	Purpose
Stage: 4- School Age **Ages: 6- 12**	Industry	Inferiority	Competency
Stage: 5- Adolescence **Ages: 13-21**	Identity	Role Confusion	Fidelity
Stage: 6- Early Adulthood **Ages: 22-39**	Intimacy	Isolation	Love
Stage: 7- Adulthood **Ages: 40-65**	Generativity	Stagnation	Care
Stage: 8- Old Age **Ages: 65- Older**	Ego Integrity	Despair	Wisdom

Based on my own interpretation of the research, these dilemmas are created due to the unfulfilled needs of a person's life. Erickson's theory does not require completion of the stage in order to advance to the next stage.[lxxxiii] In short, time continues to move forward, and life continues to happen whether the individual's needs have been fulfilled or not. So, if the need remains and is unfulfilled, the dilemma will progress on to the next stage of life and will remain until replaced by a virtue.

Unfulfilled needs must be identified and reconciled, or else the issue remains unresolved. Leaving these issues unresolved interferes with the individual's ability to find true integrity and obtain the virtue of wisdom, which according to Maslow's Theory, is self-actualization.[lxxxiv,lxxxv]

Correlation of Maslow & Erickson

Figure 4- I will refer to this model in a later chapter but it is important to show you here for the point I am trying to make.

Inability to obtain the virtues contribute to psychological and spiritual frustration. Exposure to Childhood Sexual Abuse and domestic violence which is most common during the school age and adolescent years has the potential to disorient the woman's sense of industry and identity. The dilemma is that the virtues of competency and fidelity are skewed or never fully developed, which causes a domino effect on the remaining stages of life.

Unresolved issues created by trauma are likened to voids created by destruction and devastation; which are likened to the 'muddy puddles' metaphor used earlier in this work. The voids – those potholes of life, dug by the jack hammers which have been allowed to damage us - are filled with elements of tears, feelings of inferiority, and role confusion, and if they remain unresolved, they lead to isolation. Isolation, which is like that broken pew in the back corner of the postmodern urban church in the neighborhood, filled with confusion and discomfort.

Intimacy is the ability for a person to fuse his or her identity with someone else's without the fear of losing a part of his or herself.[lxxxvi] It is one of the virtues to be gained. How often can that happen, if the person is struggling with trauma from his or her child and adolescent years? How often are there chances for intimacy when a woman who has been abused is unable to pass the virtues to her children and the generations around them. It is likened to driving on a road called life and often derailed by muddy psychological puddles. It would seem, metaphorically, that every time we gained a few miles, suddenly, *"we hit a ditch in the road."*

While the focus of this work is on women of color, we must keep in mind that men of color are affected by the same set of unresolved issues when it comes to the topic of intimacy especially in heterosexual relationships. In the definition of intimacy, is important to recognize its sexual connotation, especially toward women who have suffered and survived Childhood Sexual Abuse. The broader scope of the definition of intimacy does not isolate itself to sexual encounters. The focus in Erikson's theory also states that "those whose identities are weak and unformed will engage in relationships that will remain shallow, and the individual will experience a sense of loneliness and isolation," regardless of gender.[lxxxvii] As a result we find our communities and churches engaging in shallow relationships, looking for fulfilment with sexual encounters that lack authenticity and virtue-resulting in more dilemmas.

This identity development crisis is a major contributor to the mental health disorders listed above. In my opinion, most people who remain in a cycle of identity crisis feed the numbers of the mental illness population, which as a result generates revenue for the health care industry. In depth, what the medical industry considered a personality disorder, is a result from behaviors developed improperly possibly from genetic inheritance. Meaning, that for those whose dilemmas remained unresolved, such as the woman in the broken pew of the postmodern urban church, more money is spent in connection to a diagnosis with some form of behavioral disorder by a mental health institution. Regardless of the diagnosis, these mood and personality disorders are some of the end results of an improperly developed identity.[lxxxviii]

3.5 Resolution

Individuals who have suffered Childhood Sexual Abuse look at new adult situations through the lens of their past. I cannot emphasize enough that genetics and generational inheritances play a role in response behaviors which shape our identities as a community today. By doing this, and thus following the same behavioral patterns of the past, doubts and the fate of the unfavorable outcomes are validated and affirmed. This is possibly because of the damage to the limbic system, due to the over production of stress hormones, which causes the individual to repeat behaviors learned in the past, because he or she is unable to create new memories. These methods become psychological and theological tools which shape and mold their personalities, behaviors, and identities in the community and social setting. When left unattended, the difficulty for the person to reconcile the dilemmas and obtain virtues increases. Needs are falsely fulfilled, with institutionalized counseling, sterilized therapy, unexplained (undefined) diagnosis, and generic drug prescriptions. Not to mention that the social side of these needs are met with promiscuity, shallow relationships and isolation.

Erikson's theory affirms that if an individual does not deal with the dilemmas presented at any given stage of his or her life, then it has the potential to perpetuate toxic behavior and detrimental outcomes. The tools become toxic and useless; "tools that are no longer useful."[lxxxix] So where does that leave the responsibility of the Church? Does the postmodern urban church have a responsibility to satisfy the needs of these abused women of color, their men and their children? (No, I do not believe that is full the burden of the church alone.)

However, the postmodern urban church does have the responsibility to provide access to the necessary tools and virtues someone might need to answer the dilemmas of their life's circumstances. The question must first be rephrased and asked differently- does the postmodern urban church have the capacity to provide the tools required for the woman in the broken pew, to reconcile unresolved issues, or will she simply be pointed to some random pew, in a random section of the sanctuary?

Chapter Four:
Balancing the Books

4.1 The Negative Balance

Based on the information provided in the previous section, women affected by Trauma-based Psycho-Spiritual Disorientation have difficulty reconciling the unbalanced polarization of their dilemmas. The unbalanced polarization of the church is a result of *Triune oppression*. For the purpose of this discussion, the word triune is in reference to the Trinity, which points to the consubstantial nature of God. Triune oppression is when the knowledge of the source of creation, the word emanated from that source, and the spirit that activates and illuminates the source within the human consciousness, is denied or replaced with false consciousness or false truth imitating authentic spiritual authority.

Revisit the earlier portion of this book a re-read the story of the little girl whose father used scripture to molest her, notice how he oppressed her access to the very tool he used to manipulate her. He did not want her to attend the church anymore, nor did he allow her access to the bible or, family members who represented God in her life. He refused her any access to the consubstantial nature of the God she loved. The consubstantial nature of

God, when it is oppressed, is not limited to the physiological realm. It is internal, psychological, and spiritual. Often the results of the oppression, as well as the outcries for relief manifest itself in the physical realm. She began fighting in school. She had outbursts of anger. As a result, the triune oppression coupled with the spiritual and psychological trauma began to accumulate dilemmas rather than virtues in her life. Imagine how this woman responded when she walked in to the sanctuary of the postmodern urban church in her neighborhood. What did she see that made her more uncomfortable, so much so, that she sat down during worship?

In some postmodern, urban church settings, behaviors such as running, dancing, bucking, and falling out are interpreted as physical signs of psychological and spiritual warfare, or movements of the spirit. Some congregations would disagree that this is true based on the cultural norms of their social context. There are certain arenas where what some cultures would consider running, dancing, and shouting aloud, extreme or abnormal behavior; whereas others would consider it a necessity. Rather than debate on if these actions are an authentic move of the spirit, my focus is on the spiritual and psychological needs of the individual and whether or not the atmosphere of worship is conducive to allow God to meet that need.

Based on all we have researched and read thus far, we can safely say that with the outcry, regardless of its display is for relief of spiritual and psychological oppression, which comes from an unfulfilled and unreconciled need. Reconciling is not limited to the external model of relationships, but a "personal reconciling" of what has happened to them. When the words, such as "need, fulfillment, dilemmas, and virtues," are thrown out into the atmosphere and have created a disorientation in life- I believe, a certain level of spiritual balancing, and psychological recalibrating needs to take place. The needs must be met with adequacy, dilemmas must be resolved, and exchanged for virtues. For every stage of life there must be reconciling, on a spiritual and psychological level, otherwise the individual will identify his or her life as being filled with burden or lack, and when polarized- both.

4.2 Reconciling and Reconciliation

There are two ways to define the word *reconciling*. One definition is stated as "a process of making a view or belief consistent or compatible with another toward the restoration of friendly relations."[xc] This definition has more to do with the word reconciliation rather than reconciling. In a philosophical view, reconciliation anchors itself in the concept of ideas, narratives, persons, groups, and God.[xci]

Reconciling, however, is also an accounting process that uses two sets of records to ensure figures are accurate and in agreement.[xcii] Reconciliation as it pertains to accounting; is the key process used to determine whether the money leaving an account matches the amount spent. This practice ensures the two values balance at the end of the recording period. While the terms are different, they can be psychologically interpreted in the accounting method that before we as individuals can involve ourselves in the process of reconciliation; we must first be reconciled with ourselves. There must be an even exchange with the information, effort, and energy going out as there is coming in.

Self-assessments and reflections are necessary to get to what Maslow calls self- actualization, Erikson's theory points the way to pinpoint and process the unresolved dilemmas in life so that this woman who is sitting in the isolated section of the postmodern urban church could get to the place where she believed she needed to be. Reconciliation among moral theorist pertains to "the aftermath of everyday forms of wrongdoing such as transgressions within friendships and family relationships."[xciii] The question proposed is whether reconciliation can happen without forgiveness.[xciv] Theorists offer the concept of reconciliation without forgiveness as a positive way to move forward in difficult cases.[xcv] However is this a requirement for the social structures of the postmodern urban church? Is there a consensus in the culture of this trauma infused postmodernity of theology that perpetuates a generational behavior which responds negatively to the "forgive and forget' methods of coping with trauma? Does the culture of the church still expect the women in the broken pews to sit in silence and acceptance of both the polarization of its social context and pluralistic ignorance?

By identifying and naming the dilemmas of domestic violence and Childhood Sexual Abuse (and any other traumatic experiences), women and men who are willing to be truthful about their dilemmas will find solace, acceptance and liberation and sanctuary in sanctuaries of true and authentic worship. The postmodern urban church must become a place where women (and men) of color are able to identify themselves, forgive themselves, and forgive others. Again, this is not the full burden of the church as an institution, but it is the purpose of the church as its ecclesial mission. The church must become a place where there is an opportunity to balance the books.

4.3 Reconciling through Forgiveness

According to L. Gregory Jones, forgiving and forgetting are two very different psychological dynamics.[xcvi] "Theorists who defend the political and moral value of reconciliation more often reject the claim that reconciliation requires forgetting. Instead, these defenders generally claim that knowledge and acknowledgement of wrongdoing, as well as recognition of the victims, are crucial to successful reconciliation."[xcvii] It becomes a method of revisiting life's dilemmas and searching for a remedy, a virtue to be obtained that will completely satisfy the psycho- spiritual debt left from areas of abuse.

The secular institutions such as mental health clinics, psychiatrist and psychoanalysis professionals can respond topically by offering psychiatric drugs to suppress physiological/behavioral manifestations triggered by memories of domestic violence, child sexual abuse, and any other traumatic instances. Rather than reconcile, or balance the books, by removing the unnecessary psychological weight on the one side of the scale, it places more weight on the opposite side creating a heavier burden, and a false balancing.

Return to the idea of polarization in contrast to consubstantiality. The mistake that the church has made is that it has adopted the institutional model- only one method of treatment- when responding to individuals [especially women] who are attempting to reconcile their dilemmas created by Psycho-Spiritual Disorientation created by the trauma of triune oppression. The alternative is the ecclesial response, which grants permission and encourages bouts of emotionally charged behavior without addressing the underlying cause of the dilemma. The church as both an institution and ecclesial body must remember that God's forgiveness and reconciliation are not isolated to psychological or cognitive reasoning but are essentially rooted in the matters of the spirit.

Rather than completely taking away the God

centeredness of forgiveness and reconciliation, the postmodern urban church culture has provided a flimsy substitute. The substitution is, in my opinion, far worse than triune oppression; it is triune substitution. The leaders, such as preachers, pastors, and teachers of the ecclesial church become the participants in psycho-spiritual abuse when they refuse to search out, reveal, name, and articulate the lament attached to the process of reconciling. It is like a spiritual yolk around the neck of those who are already handcuffed and oppressed. It is like placing a noose on the neck of a slave already captured and beaten- as if the reason for running away was not traumatizing enough. Has the postmodern urban church become slave masters to those oppressed by silence in the presence of God and replacing God with this flimsy substitution of unauthentic clichés and emotionalism? Has it, captured with dogmas, oppressed with schisms, and abused with clichés, the women who walk through the doors looking who are making the attempt to find freedom from inferiority? Has it withheld access to the needed virtues of life hope, will, purpose, competency, fidelity, love, care, and wisdom, because it refuses to acknowledge and articulate the need?

When the culture of the postmodern urban church suppresses the reconciling power of

God's word within the congregation in order to maintain emotional control, the leaders have simply re-victimized those who are already traumatized. Spiritual suppression is accomplished by quieting both the individual lament, the communal lament of the people who are dealing with trauma based psychological and spiritual disorientation, and God's participation in both.

So, how should the postmodern urban church respond? How can the church help those who are spiritually over calculating or overcompensating their life's dilemmas so that they can balance the books? How can the as church equip itself to become more consubstantial in its polarized approach?

Jones outlined six steps to forgiveness: I have modified the direction of the language he uses to make the conversation flow toward women of color.[xcviii] Hopefully the outline provided in these steps will help the church to create an atmosphere of healing and forgiveness. The reason these steps are important for both the communal and personal lament of women [and men] of color is because it provides an opportunity to articulate, in the presence of God, willingness to offer and receive reconciliation for every crisis, dilemma, spiritual and psychological need.

First, the [woman] must first be willing to speak

truthfully and patiently about the conflict in his or her life. She must confront the memories rather than suppress them. Then she must acknowledge the emotions of anger and bitterness and be willing to overcome them.[xcix] The ability to identify and articulate the psychological and spiritual needs of the woman are the first steps toward the process of healing. Creating an atmosphere where the woman can confront the memories of her past and acknowledge the emotions she is experiencing, are only the initial movements toward reaching the point of self-actualization.

Secondly It is essential that the person who desires healing, responds [or is encouraged to respond] with honesty. Often, people fear articulating this feeling of anger because of the discomforts placed on them by their immediate social circles. This could be the very reason that many women often shut down or refuse to express the emotions they are experiencing. They risk being called crazy, or dysfunctional, or being labeled with a disorder by those in their communities. Those who are new to the institutions, especially those of the church, seem encouraged to suppress their anger, because of a false notion, that to articulate their dissatisfaction with God is pejorative by the postmodern church's social norm.

The third step is that she must realize that the offender is also a child of God and be concerned for the other person's wellness.[c] My disclaimer is that realizing that the offender is a child of God does not dismiss holding them accountable for their actions. The lament for God to hold the abusers accountable is necessary in the atmosphere of worship. The reason is because it will bring the woman to the fourth step- seeing God in the other. She must be willing to recognize the complicity in both personal and situational conflicts. Her perspective considers the steps that were required to foster forgiveness for her abuser, her community, and repentance for herself.[ci]

The last two steps are that, she makes a decision and a commitment to change the behavior that perpetuates conflict and crimes against his or herself and/ or another person and continues to confess the actualization of reconciliation with God. Cultivating a lifestyle of healthy self-examination, with the proper spiritual and psychological tools fosters behavioral changes and ability to attaining the necessary virtues of life. Although some issues take longer to reconcile or resolve, faith in the possibility of total restoration through the power of Truth becomes the generativity needed to continue the process of healing.

4.4 The Reconciling Gospel Truth

According to Jones, confessing a yearning for

reconciliation is one of the final steps in the process of forgiveness. In the postmodern urban church, confession is the articulation of the *Gospel Truth*.[cii] This introduces us to the task of the womanist pastor or preacher of the Gospel within the social context of the postmodern urban church. Many womanist preachers have experienced some form of Trauma-based Psycho-Spiritual Disorientation. Womanists must be careful not to proclaim a gospel based on a theology that makes the victims of trauma responsible for unearthing the hidden meaning of trauma.[ciii] The only responsibility of both the preacher and parishioner is to articulate the truth, and the spirit of Truth will reveal the meaning. Truth is an element used to bring balance "the books."

Proclaiming a gospel full of emotion, and absent of theological truth as it pertains to suffering, is the type of message that would re-violate the survivor of any kind of trauma, and cause re-injury to the emotional and mental state of the individual.[civ]Why?, Because emotional atmospheres will not reconcile dilemmas, they only retrigger the limbic system so that the woman remembers instances where she was abused. If our preaching does not provide access to virtues, the risk is that the hearers leave the sanctuary without reconciliation or an opportunity to heal. If the postmodern urban church culture responds with emotional trigger words, clichés and other forms of emotional stimuli to the spiritual and psychological needs proposed and articulated, it risks becoming a community dependent on the emotional high as though it is a narcotic drug or a prescription.

Based on the behavioral research provided, it is safe to make the statement that these women, who attend church attempting to reconcile, recalibrate, and re-orient, the disorientation suffered from spiritual and psychological trauma, are susceptible to becoming addicted to the temporary fulfillment of their emotional needs. As a result, the church is burdened with the expectation of producing emotional satisfaction on a weekly basis. Preaching a biblical hermeneutic filled with inanities, and rhetoric, which does not equip the listeners with the theological tools to initiate psychological change, is useless. It creates a burden for both the atmosphere of the church and the people who attend. Maybe, that is why the woman sat down during worship. Is it possible that although the program said *"worship,"* it had been replaced with emotionalism and a false sense of healing? Was the inauthenticity so prevalent in the room that it triggered a heavier burden and a false balancing to her spiritual and psychological scale? I wonder. I think this woman needed someone who would articulate the way she was feeling, the abuse she had suffered with empathy and authenticity. As we get ready to shift into the need of womanist preaching, I hope I have set the stage for the type of congregation womanist preachers minister to and the struggles we are facing in the age of postmodernity.

On the other hand, keep in mind that people to whom womanist preachers minister do not live their lives in a world of technological marvels; their lives are not symmetrical, nor are they as chronological as our well-prepared exegetic sermons.[cv] The people we, womanist preachers, minister to are dealing with moral, emotional, and spiritual turmoil at any given stage of their lives. Similarly, the womanist preacher -who is also subject to human nature - is also dealing with spiritual, emotional, and moral dilemmas as well.

4.5 The Womanist Preacher

James Forbes in his book, *The Holy Spirit and Preaching,* states, "Unless [the preacher] finds the courage to share what his or her pilgrimage has been and what he or she has been called to do, the anointing *of preaching* cannot be realized."[cvi] In his book, *Otherwise Preaching,* McClure states "it is important that we not only constantly compare our conclusions with the teachings of scripture, but that we also compare them with the facts of existence."[cvii] Leslie Newbigin affirms this concept by suggesting that "in presenting the Gospel message, we must understand that facts [alone] do not have the power, by themselves to imprint on the brain."[cviii] The facts must be presented, grasped, processed, and understood, before being accepted as the Gospel Truth.

The goal of womanist preaching is that its perspectives use a language that articulates oppression and liberation in a way that presents the gospel in a way that will be received by the audience in hope that it will help someone to heal. The facts must remain in order to protect the mysteries of faith from the reductionism of scientific rationality otherwise preachers will become content to settle for an ever-narrowing faith-history.

The function of preaching and confrontation with the revealed word of God is to increase our abilities to raise the hidden word of God into consciousness.[cix] For womanist preachers, propositions cannot be reduced to sentences, and automatically accepted by the naysayers in the masses we preach to. The propositions presented must articulate expressions of possibility that belong to the mental poll of all experience.[cx] One of the ways we reach our audiences is by offering biblical proposals for imaginative reflection.[cxi] "Process preachers should teach process theology itself from the pulpit as a novel reconstruction of biblical information and contemporary experience."[cxii] Storytelling becomes the central nature of our preaching. Could this be because telling the story, triggers the emotion, and creates or applies truth to both new and past memories?

Storytelling creates an atmosphere that gives a voice to the voiceless. When we tell the true story of our suffering, it breaks the silence of the broken pews. It causes the search for healing to become consubstantial and not merely one-sided. It changes the dynamics of how the believer sees God. No longer does it seem as though God is not willing to meet the individual at his or her point of need. The story shows through image and metaphor, that the God of Creation, the Word, and the Spirit of the word, which is ready like a healing balm to be applied, and reconcile any dilemma, any crises, any question, relieve any burden, identify and remove useless tools. It causes the church to become a regime of mediation.

4.6 The Regime of Mediation

Women who suffer from Trauma-based Psycho-Spiritual disorientation naturally look for a focal point to place blame for traumatic episodes in life. It is a part an attempt of revisiting memories in the past in order to reconcile dilemmas and obtain virtues. Sometimes revisiting these memories are involuntary and blame impulsively placed where it does not belong. Is it unfair to place blame where it does not belong; on God, for not intervening, or on the victim for some form of disobedience to God? If we replaced the word "blame," with the word "accountability" would that change the perception?

The womanist theological teaching must provide survivors of abuse the ability to hold abusers accountable for their actions. The blame belongs on the fact that human beings have the potential to choose whether they will or will not commit acts of abuse. It must incorporate a theologically therapeutic method of proclamation for people, especially women of color, who have endured abuse and oppression, to find a point of reference to meet God the creator, the Word, and Spirit. The church and its leaders must present the gospel in a manner that is therapeutic, truthful, liberating, and not cultic and increasingly oppressive.[cxiii]

Could it be that the women who enter the sanctuaries of the postmodern urban church desire to hear the truth that speaks about their current life circumstances? Do they desire to hear that there is hope of recovery, redemption, and restoration from their brokenness? While the womanist preacher could easily use her experiences as the proof of that hope; it will not suffice as the kind of power or authority needed for the conversion of the non-believer. "By broadening the definition of experience to include an organic feeling of awareness beyond what is available in the symbols given to human consciousness, [womanist] theologians sought to raise into awareness a non-sensory form of knowledge that could include spiritual realities such as God, Christ, word of God, and so on."[cxiv]In short, the subjective truth of our experiences are not enough, our stories must align and include with the truth of God's Word in order for being effective.

According to James Forbes, as it pertains to preaching, "The preaching event itself-without reference to specific text and themes-is a living, breathing, flesh and blood expression, of the theology of the Holy Spirit." [cxv] It fosters an atmosphere for healing.[cxvi] He states, "The preaching event is an aspect of the broader work of the Spirit to nurture, empower, and guide the church [and its parishioners] in order that it may serve the kingdom of God in the power of the Spirit.[cxvii] In our secular, postmodern age, [womanist preachers] risk appearing unsophisticated if there is too much talk about a spiritual dimension of reality, or if we make too much space for the presence and activity of the Spirit in our day – to – day experiences... sometimes ecclesiastical leaders fear that private and personal spiritual visitations will lead to excess and potential conflict in the community of believers."[cxviii] While this is a fair assumption, women have a need to be allowed an opportunity to articulate and express their needs for relief from Trauma- based Psycho-Spiritual Disorientation.

The Spirit of Truth is always knocking at the door of our hearts, with a desire to lead and guide us in the ways that we should go. It is the initiator of Mediation. It invites us to the table of fellowship and articulation. The indwelling of the Holy Spirit comes immediately to those who answer the call to fellowship with Christ and accept the redeeming love of God, which comes through belief, confession, and obedience.[cxix] Identifying the church as a mediator for the wounded to find refuge from the pain inflicted from the mechanisms of the world involves understanding that the church culture, which has a history dealing with oppression and abuse, is attributed the title of being a place where God will fulfill the need. The Church then becomes what institutional agencies would consider an agent of a therapeutic community.[cxx]

There are three spiritual practices which are unique to the church experience; exhortation, prayer, and testimony. These as methods of worship that have existed for women since the 19th Century. These spiritual practices correlate to the positive mental health status of who have endured social and spiritual oppression, hence, African American women [and men].[cxxi]

The Holy Spirit does not arrive as though it is a reward for good behavior, or perfect incantations, or good deeds toward God, but it is a gift of God, from God, to help the believers understand the truth regardless of race, gender, or class. The womanist preacher must to preach the Gospel of Christ, inclusive of the Holy Spirt, Biblical history, and life experience. All three of these elements are needed so that those who will receive the preached message of the gospel will find useful tools that reconcile their life's dilemmas.

Now that we have an understanding about the right of women [especially women of color], to preach the gospel under the power of the Holy Spirit, let us move forward to the worship experience for both the womanist preacher and the congregation she serves. As stated previously in this dissertation, the congregation is not isolated to a building or institution, but it is an ecclesial body of people who share in the faith of Christ and is welcoming of those who desire to have a relationship with God through Christ. To foster this type of atmosphere, the womanist response is necessary for those who are suffering from Trauma-based Psycho- Spiritual disorientation. The method of the womanist response is likened to and through the solidarity of what psychologists call a Talking Cure.

Chapter Five:
Worship is Therapeutic-
A Corporate Talking
Cure

5.1 The Voice of Lament

According to Walter C. Kaiser Jr., "two broad categories of genres in the Old Testament are prose and poetry."[cxxii] Since the early days of form criticism the biblical laments have been divided into two categories, to distinguish whether the lament is from a single individual or if it represents the issues that were present in the community.[cxxiii] Here we should discern how individual and communal lament both have a direct effect on the self-actualization of the individual suffering with Psycho-Spiritual Disorientation. Looking at an individual suffering with Psycho-Spiritual Disorientation, the individual may reach a level of self-actualization through a five-tier model of human needs. These tiers are not isolated to age groupings such as in Erik Erikson's *Theory of Adult Development.* Below I have correlated Erickson's Theory with Maslow's theory to show that as a woman progresses through life each need increases with complexity. This model is also articulated in the figure 3 of this work.[cxxiv]

Correlation of Maslow & Erickson

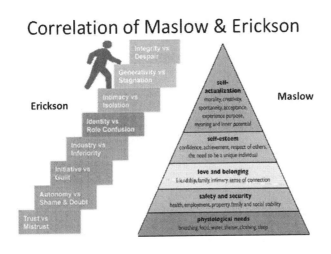

Figure 5 - Side by side comparison of Erikson's Adult Development, and Maslow's Needs Hierarchy.[cxxv]

So why is this model important to the voice of lament? Per Kaiser, lament is a cry to fulfill a need. People cry out to have their needs fulfilled. Whatever stage in life the individual finds his or herself in will determine the cry out and what kind of needs they have.[cxxvi] Maslow's theory pertains to the need for lament. For Maslow, a person is always "becoming" and never remains static."[cxxvii]

Self-actualized people seek fulfillment that is only quenched when they are doing all they are capable of.

Unfortunately, the process that leads to the fulfillment of self-actualization is disrupted or disoriented by life experiences at the lower level of needs.[cxxviii] Below is another model I created to illustrate the needs of women who suffer with hormonal and mood behaviors which create disorientation. As we compare Phelps' model of mood and behavior, pertaining to the hormone fluctuations of women, and Maslow's Hierarchy of needs, we realize that women have needs that reoccur at every stage of life on a continuous cycle. For every dilemma presented for women of color there is an additional layer of psychological struggles added to the equation. The model proposes that the appropriate responses are in Maslow's Hierarchy of needs theory.

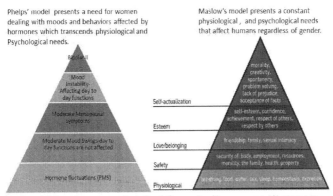

Correlation of Phelps' Mood & Behavior Pyramid, to Maslow's Hierarchy of Needs

Phelps' model presents a need for women dealing with moods and behaviors affected by hormones which transcends physiological and Psychological needs.

Maslow's model presents a constant physiological, and psychological needs that affect humans regardless of gender.

Bipolar II

Mood instability- Affecting day to day functions

Moderate Menopausal symptoms

Moderate Mood Swings-day to day functions are not affected

Hormone fluctuations (PMS)

Self-actualization

Esteem

Love/belonging

Safety

Physiological

morality, creativity, spontaneity, problem solving, lack of prejudice, acceptance of facts

self-esteem, confidence, achievement, respect of others, respect by others

friendship, family, sexual intimacy

security of body, employment, resources, morality, the family, health, property

breathing, food, water, sex, sleep, homeostasis, excretion

This model's intent is to represent the duality of dilemmas faced by women, especially women of color. Maslow's Theory correlates a response to each level of Phelps' Mood & Behavior Pyramid.

Figure 6 – Correlation of Phelps' Mood & Behavior Pyramid to Maslow's Hierarchy of Needs

There is a deep need for lament, because the need to be satisfied at the top of Maslow's hierarchical structure is not physiological, but spiritual. According to the pyramid, self-actualization is beyond the psychological needs of a person; therefore, to satisfy a salient need for growth, a person must engage in an activity that will satisfy the need. In this way, lament is the cry used to satisfy the need for growth. However, when we add Phelps' mood and behavior pyramid, we understand that there is a duality of need and an increase on psychological heaviness for women, especially women who have experienced the traumatization of Childhood

Sexual Abuse, or any other form of domestic violence, and have not received access to the proper treatments. Lament then becomes an outcry for preventative care for women who have suffered in silence for prolonged periods and have reached a level of need that goes beyond a physiological remedy. At the psychological level, both the mood behavior model and hierarchy of needs model shows that women especially need to have an atmosphere where a sense of love and belonging, encouragement and self-esteem are accessible to them.

According to Kaiser, "laments run the gamut of emotions, from complaints, to protestations of innocence, to praise to God for his deliverance.[cxxix] Lamentations are designed to acknowledge the hurt and give the wounded a voice to articulate it in the presence of God. It is in those places of spiritual disorientation, that we need to refocus our attention toward the source of our spiritual being so that our perspectives are clarified, and a movement toward self-actualization is made. The issue is that in our humanity—engulfed by postmodernist thinking—we have tried to satisfy a spiritual need with physiological remedies, and as a result perpetuating psychological frustration.

In his discussion on the Psalms of disorientation, Walter Brueggemann says:

> "It is a curious fact that the church has, by and large, continued to sing songs of orientation in a world increasingly experienced as disorientation

... It is my judgement that this action of the church is less an evangelical defiance guided by faith, and much more a frightened, numb denial and deception that does not want to acknowledge or experience the disorientation of life."[cxxx]

This phrase by Bruggeman captures the polarization of the church in the separation of the institution from the ecclesial. Postmodernity separates the communal laments from the individual laments and widens the gaps between them by singing songs of happiness in the face of sorrow. Brueggemann says this kind of behavior is "very different from what the Bible itself does."[cxxxi]

Womanist theological views agree with Brueggemann when he states that "in every successful and affluent culture, it is believed that enough power and knowledge can tame the terror and eliminate the darkness." Darkness, then, is likened to prolonged psychological and spiritual disorientation and its existence attests to the resilience of it in spite of our cognitive reasoning.[cxxxii]

Erikson, in his Identity Development Theory, affirms that if an individual does not deal with the dilemmas encountered at any given stage of his or her life, they have the potential to perpetuate toxic behavior and detrimental outcomes.[cxxxiii] As we take a look at the comparison model above (fig.6) we notice the default of women who's self -actualization needs remain unfulfilled. A cumulative perspective of the model suggests that at each stage proposed by Erickson, a self-actualization or virtue must be attained, if not Tools become toxic and useless, and "there is no greater burden than a tool that is no longer useful."[cxxxiv]

Statistics implicate that the majority of people who undergo traumatic abuse early in life, such as child sexual abuse and domestic violence, endure a lifetime finding emotional, physical, and spiritual healing.[cxxxv] Private social agencies tend to exclude those who have personal troubles—those with whom they have the least success treating.[cxxxvi] Successful treatment requires the person to come to a sense of closure through forgiveness and to take steps toward changing his or her response to their traumatic history; yet the overall economic status of the under-privileged population that determines whether certain individuals receive necessary care. This kind of economic separation contributes to the neglect received by the "poorer class" from the healthcare industry.[cxxxvii]

Sigmund Freud, the father of psychoanalysis, performed studies that will anchor the focus of this work as it pertains to the Womanist response to the psychological and spiritual traumas of Psycho-Spiritual Disorientation, which comes as a result of triune oppression. One Bertha Pappenheim, who was presented under the name Anna O, was named as the original patient of Freud's psychoanalytic therapy—called The Talking Cure.[cxxxviii] While conversion disorder (which is psychosomatic), and other terms related to the history of psychoanalysis with Anna O are at the center of the conversation, for the purposes of this report my focus is on the talking cure in relationship to the voice of lament, which lends itself to treating Psycho-Spiritual Disorientation caused by triune oppression.

The Talking Cure, according to the *Psychology Dictionary*, is a therapeutic practice where the client is asked to speak freely and without judgment so that the therapist can diagnose the problem and recommend treatment options.[cxxxix] This therapeutic method links itself to psychosomatic pain, which is also relative to childhood development. Here again, Erikson's theory of adult development and Maslow's Hierarchy of Needs (Growth) inform a connection between the therapeutic nature and necessity of the consubstantiation of Christ's Church.

Stephen L. Salter, in his article *Return of the Talking Cure: Finding Words for Chronic Pain,* validates the reason that lament is necessary for healing:

> All children long to be loved and accepted, safe and contained. When those needs are met with rejection, frustration, or intolerance, the child becomes quite shy with regard to her needs. She loses the opportunity to put feelings into language . . . because that capability requires the nurturing of a caregiver in order to develop. The child understands her feelings as unacceptable.

Since she still needs to maintain her relationship with her caregiver, she attempts to get rid of them, feeling her caregiver doesn't want them. She represses them.[cxl]

Combine the story of the unresolved issues, to the story of the broken pew and we will find Salter speaks to this type of trauma, saying:

"She continues to repress them as she develops because she has never learned how to process them. Her efforts to 'get rid' of her needs usually result in her treating herself poorly. For instance, responding to the demands of life, she may place severe pressure on herself, beat herself up, terrify herself—sometimes incessantly—all day long— and every day. Because she is unable to articulate her feelings, they will reside as bodily symptoms, at times as chronic pain. Chronic pain may manifest as headaches, neck pain, fibromyalgia, joint pain, back pain, and so on."[cxli]

As stated in Erikson's Identity Development Theory, if an individual does not deal with the dilemmas encountered at any given stage of his or her life, they have the potential to perpetuate toxic behavior and detrimental outcomes, in turn, repression becomes the radius for psychosomatic illnesses. Repressed feelings and denial of articulation due to societal oppression have the ability to create pain that is spiritually destabilizing, psychologically disorienting, and physiologically manifesting. In most urban cultures of the postmodern church, movements of the Spirit are interpreted as people running around the sanctuary, screaming, dancing and crying. The greater question the church should perhaps ask is what amounts of chronic pain, depression, and are psychosomatic. Is the church the same as the institutions who profit from mistreating curable diseases? Does the church share that same guilt of withholding the *Talking Cure*?

5.2 Worship as the Articulation of Suffering

The spiritual practice of worship is inclusive of all of the spiritual practices mentioned above. In this unique spiritual exercise, worship assists the wounded by providing a place of praise to God, expressing his or her heritage, and demanding respect for justice, human freedom, and dignity. Worship provides the articulation of suffering and gives the victim the ability to name the problem. Prayer and testimony are both a part of the complete worship experience. Then the sanctuaries of our postmodern urban churches become the places where the need for God's healing; sustaining, guidance, and reconciliation are not only desired but also received.[cxlii]

In worship, those affected by Trauma-based Psycho-Spiritual Disorientation can receive satisfying intervention without the restrictions and prejudices of the authorities and legal systems that have failed them in the past.[cxliii] It is an opportunity for personal and direct communication with God. In a communal setting, worship becomes a therapeutic environment in which enables survivors to name their emotions in response to their problems. When the place of worship is prepared, on either an individual or communal setting, the survivor has access to receive the soothing balm of the Gospel message. This message assures her of God's love through the suffering of Christ.[cxliv] While no one individual is responsible for making the worship experience conducive for healing, those who have been elected to leadership positions within the church as both an institution and ecclesial body, have the charge to encourage, and conduct an atmosphere which invites the Spirit of Truth to be present among the people. As previously implied, the atmosphere of worship is not a substitute for medical treatment, but a consubstantial approach to wellness and holistic healing.

For a person who is trying to find the meaning of his or her suffering, the place of worship is a place to remember, and associate his or her suffering to the suffering of Christ. This association makes the worship experience a response of God, toward aiding the survivor. It reveals and releases those who have been victimized by *triune oppression.*[cxlv] The church, its leadership, and a working theological hermeneutic, is the therapeutic agent for an individual to find the truth about, reconcile the meaning of, and give a voice to the abuse and oppression they have suffered with. In the congregational settings of worship, there is an urgency to resolve the dilemmas which have been suppressed through each stage of his or her identity development. According to Erikson's theory, starting the recovery process depends heavily on when the crossroads of suffering and redemptive truth meet.

Keep in mind that there are some people who have intertwined religion and violence, and it has left them with theological questions on faith, quietism, and complicity.[cxlvi] This requires a precise use of scripture to separate the cultic mindset of violence, and religion. Hebrews 4:12 states "For the word of God is living and active. Sharper than any double-edged sword, it pierces even to dividing soul and spirit, joints and marrow. It is able to judge the thoughts and intentions of the heart."[cxlvii] Just as a hospital, its doctors, its nurses and staff are prepared for open heart surgery, removal of cancerous tumors removed with precision instruments, or the birth of a baby, metaphorically the church must be ready to respond in the same manner.

The task of the church is to mediate an atmosphere of forgiveness, by allowing the full expression of remembrance. This remembrance is not unaided but nurtured in remembrance of the suffering in Christ. The Womanist preacher has the task of being theologically trained in responding to survivors of

Childhood Sexual Abuse and Domestic Violence with the understanding that the processes of God do not require the survivor to simply forgive and forget, 'get over it,' and it's all better.[cxlviii] Recalling Gregory Jones' statement; *"forgiving and forgetting are two totally different psychological dynamics,"*[cxlix] The word must be preached with precision and used as a surgeon's scalpel to separate the guilt from the pain. The womanist preacher must also be willing to remember, revisit and re-forgive based on her own experiences. This act enables her to draw from the well of Truth and pour out into the life of those who are thirsting for an articulation of their suffering. She can use her own truth to draw, but she must use God's *Truth* to pour out.[cl]

5.3 Preaching as an Articulation of Theocentric Therapy

For the last portion of this chapter, I want to close with the importance of womanist preaching- not only to the congregation- but to the womanist herself. The preacher and the congregation need some sense of the Spirit accompanied by power sufficient to interrupt a decline in this sense of the reality of God.[cli] If womanist preachers intend to preach the gospel of Jesus the Christ, who calls us to serve the kingdom in our time, we need all the power that is available to us… mere ranting and raving and excitation from some spirited woman pastor will not suffice."

In all instances, a major part of the homiletic task is the business of accessing lost voices within the tradition and building strong pockets of face to face communication within and across congregations and other groups."[clii] I have found that understanding womanist preaching as a form of worship is one way to gain spiritual access to the lost voices within a tradition. Herein lies the purpose of this work: *"I Hope This Helps Someone."*

The postmodern urban church community is called by God to be a community that fosters healing. The woman in the broken pew came with an expectation to enter an atmosphere that created a safe space for healing. It can create an atmosphere for spiritual and psychological healing by providing theocentric worship experiences, to those dealing with the psychological disorders resulting from Childhood Sexual Abuse and Domestic Violence. The postmodern urban church as a community collectively must understand that "long after the child has been physiologically freed, they still feel the heavy chains of despair, resentment, hopelessness, and hatred as adults.

This is because something was stolen from them that they feel they can never recover—their precious innocent childhood."[cliii]

With all this research about the disorders which

were carried throughout the young woman's life—the women in the broken pew become more understandable, in why she sat herself down on *that* broken pew *that* Sunday. There were some areas in her life that had to be re-identified—the church as an institution would not be able to respond effectively to ease the weight of these psychological and spiritual chains. She needed an encounter—a true encounter—a re-identifying encounter with an ecclesial atmosphere. The sanctuary she was looking for was not in the four walls of the institutional church. She was going to have to re-create a space for God.

She determined that the next step for her was to find not only what dilemmas in her life had not been resolved, but also the ones poorly dealt with. There is nothing physically broken with the pew, but there *is* something skewed about the atmosphere in the church. It was an atmosphere of silence surrounded by noise and movement. An atmosphere saturated with postmodernism and individuality. It had become a place where people consumed with their own story, and hardly concerned with anyone else's. The self- consumption became a type of silence within the sanctuary, although the noise of the music was blaring. It is a silence personified as someone screaming at the top of his or her lungs, in an airtight glass room—suspended in outer space. Visually seen is kicking, bucking, running in circles, making noise that everyone can see (if they are looking), but no one can hear from the outside.

Why is this? Could it be that the postmodern urban church has become increasingly narcissistic in worship? Has it made the mistake of taking the focus of worship off God and began to attend worship services to receive a blessing rather than bring an offering? [cliv] Could it be that this new generation of the postmodern urban church, has become so consumed in its own self-fulfillment, that it takes its own priority in the environment of worship, rather than any other roles and responsibilities toward God?"[clv]

The consubstantial approach eliminates the polarized responses of the church to the individual dilemmas of its parishioners, especially its women. The consubstantial approach helps both the church and its parishioners to reconcile their stigmas with the reality of Christ. The consubstantial worship experience articulates the polarization of trauma. God and God's word offers to those who are suffering spiritually and psychologically with silence and opportunity to articulate, name, lament, and confess his or her pain. It creates an atmosphere of exchange in order to reconcile unresolved issues.

Chapter Six:
Words of Encouragement
&Conclusive Thoughts

I hope that through this reading you have realized that breaking away from the spiritual bondage that we have created for ourselves is more difficult than breaking away from bondages that others have created for us. The reason it is tough is because the escape from psychological bondage involves the confrontation of information that we have embedded in our own personal psyche.

Many of us have convinced ourselves that we are to perform in a specific way so that we can be accepted by our immediate social structure. When the immediate societal structure is unstable, then finding comfort in it is difficult and presents a confrontation of information. This confrontation brings conflict. I want to suggest here that all too often we try to avoid conflict – when it comes to our own personal identity- because the conflict is [in reality] internal, not external. James 4:1 says, that the fights come from within us and are not external at all. It is not until we confront the desires within us that we will get to the place where we are able to grasp our identity. I hope that through this research you were able to find your voice, or at least a reason to have one.

In this conclusive chapter, I have added some of my sermons and reflections that have helped me through so rough situations on my own journey. I am offering them to you, with prayers and hopes that they will give you a different perspective on life. This is my personal desire that no matter where the broken pews are located, your presence, knowledge, and voice will help mend them- and at the same time yours will be fixed as well. First, I want to share these words of encouragement with you about a woman who had to push past the opinions of others, and discover her identity, by finding her faith in the word of God.

6.1 Unshackled! God's Gift to Freedom

In Luke Chapter 7, there was a woman heavily burdened with sin, and she is placed in this story at what I call "the church meeting after church," you know the dinner after church; Jesus was there, the Pharisees were there and the women who was known as a prostitute was there. She was at the feet of Jesus crying tears, and while everyone else in the church was judging her, and bringing up her past, identifying her by her circumstance and her condition, she was at the feet of Jesus, looking for something to fill the void of abuse she had endured.

Because of her condition, in their eyes, she wasn't fit to be in the church, maybe her earrings were too big, maybe her shirt was too small, maybe her skirt was too short, or her pants were too tight. Maybe she had tattoos, or a nose ring, or eyelashes were too, whatever it was, according to the people in the church, she didn't have a place in the synagogue: according to them, she wasn't a Jew. She wasn't religious. She wasn't holy. So, in the eyes of her community, she wasn't clean.

So, she would just show up, at the dinner service after church, hoping that someone would notice her and give her a chance to change her life. I can just see this woman who had taken up prostitution, most likely, she went down that road, because someone, somewhere sexually abused her, and this was the only life she knew, we don't know, but maybe she was divorced and left an abusive husband, and the only way that she could get by was to live 'this' lifestyle, we don't know, but maybe she had children at home to feed, but what we do know is that she had a box, and there were some things in that box that *reminded* her of her life and the way she had been living. It may have been all she had, that meant anything to her, it was her safety net, "just in-case" she fell on hard times, it was something that she had put her trust in to bring her through a rough patch, but it wasn't enough, because every Sunday here she was among the church folk. She was looking for acceptance, she was looking love, she was looking for forgiveness, she was looking for a word, she was looking for truth, here she was among the church folk, looking for GOD, and Sunday After Sunday, all she got, was talked about, all she got, was mistreated, all she got was abused, even more by the men in the church… all she got was the works of the flesh… but one day Christ Showed up, at the church after-party, at the church get together, and the woman, so overwhelmed by emotional poverty, so overwhelmed by spiritual poverty, so overwhelmed by physical poverty, received a word from God himself… "Your sins are forgiven." See there were so many religious people, who were using the scriptures to put the people down instead of building them up, and Jesus the human had to reach beyond himself into the spirit of Christ which dwelled in him, and the word of God had come to the woman living in a shackled state.

Then people began to question; "who is this that forgives sins?" We must realize that when the word comes through you, people will begin to question you, when you have pushed past your human nature and begin to operate in the spirit of Christ. When a word of freedom comes through you, people will try to question your motives, make you feel guilty, when the word of healing comes through you, then people begin to question your faith and look for your scars, when compassion comes through you, they try to make it perverted. And they questioned the word that the woman had received… sometimes there are people who will question you so much to the point as to where you begin to question yourself.

She was looking for acceptance in a place where she should have been received, but the people were too religious to see that she was lonely. She was looking for acceptance and reconciliation to the Truth. She was screaming silently. If we are going to be a church within society that is able to reach beyond ourselves, then we are going to have to equip ourselves with a word that can pass through the bondage that an alternative society has labeled them with. Then Jesus said to her, Your FAITH has saved you. She had received the forgiveness of the Word. She had been reconciled to God! She no longer had to hold herself hostage with the burden of guilt, but no one has shared with us the gospel of forgiveness. We continue to hold ourselves hostage, when God has already forgiven us.

In this parable, Jesus said that "the ones who love much have been forgiven much." For some reason the church has forgotten that we have been forgiven much. Is this the reason why we do not accept one another? Do we blur the lines between acceptance and approval? Let us be reminded that acceptance does not mean approval, but it means just what it is- acceptance. Acceptance is what Jesus showed in ministry to his community. Jesus began by reaching beyond his flesh, ego, and social norms, and became intentional about sharing the gospel. It is only at that moment that we follow in the example of Christ that the Truth is unshackled.

Woman of God, it is my prayer that you live your life unshackled by the Spirit of God's word and be made whole by your faith in him. It is my desire and my prayer that your psychological and spiritual needs are fulfilled by an encounter with God. Peter the apostle, says in 2 Peter 1: 5-9 states: For this very reason, make every effort to add to your faith goodness; and to goodness, knowledge; 6 and to knowledge, self-control; and to self-control, perseverance; and to perseverance, godliness; 7 and to godliness, mutual affection; and to mutual affection, love. *8 For if you possess these qualities in increasing measure, they will keep you from being ineffective and unproductive in your knowledge of our Lord Jesus Christ.* 9 But whoever does not have them is nearsighted and blind, forgetting that they have been cleansed from their past sins. Remember that you are worth God's love. God has accepted you and approved you. Also remember that God's love is more powerful than sin and it is through Christ, God will reconcile everything that has gone wrong in your life and balance your books.

Dear woman, you may have been called to lead others out of spiritual and psychological bondage. You may have received the call to leadership in ministry. I understand that there are times in your life that you will feel alone and forsaken and isolated from others people. There are going to be times where you will feel that your preaching, prayers, and ministry has fallen on deaf ears. There will be times where, you have prepared countless hours, laid awake at night, because the needs of the people seem as though they have been laid on your shoulders. It is like a heavy burden, or a cross (if you will). There are times that it will seem that you have poured out your life and your heart to see others do well, and still find yourself feeling abandoned, absconded, and attacked. It will seem as if there is no time to pray, and even if you did have the time, you would ask yourself, - "does God even hear me, and will I hear him if he answers?" Maybe this is you- Maybe. If so, I want to share with you a reflection that may give you another perspective when you are feeling this way.

6.2 Feeling Forsaken & Fulfilling the Call:
Matthew 27:45- 52a NIV

"From noon until three in the afternoon darkness came over all the land. About three in the afternoon Jesus cried out in a loud voice, *"Eli, Eli,ᶜ lemasabachthani?"* (which means "My God, my God, why have you forsaken me?"). When some of those standing there heard this, they said, "He's calling Elijah. Immediately one of them ran and got a sponge. He filled it with wine vinegar, put it on a staff, and offered it to Jesus to drink. The rest said, "Now leave him alone. Let's see if Elijah comes to save him."

And when Jesus had cried out again in a loud voice, he gave up his spirit.

At that moment the curtain of the temple was torn in two from top to bottom. The earth shook, the rocks split, and the tombs broke open.

In a sermon I wrote, I took this concept to Christ's words on the cross. It was my suggestion and view that even while Jesus was suffering and dying, he still fulfilled the call of Christ on his life. As a womanist preacher looking at this text through the lens of responding to Trauma based Psycho-Spiritual Disorientation, here is a brief reflection:

On the day that Jesus dies, there is a parade of goats, lambs, and calves going into the Temple for the Passover sacrifice. The animals are being slaughtered and the priests are catching the blood and pouring it on the altar. The people who can afford to present a sacrifice are in the temple, but what happens to the people on the outside. I see this event as both the closing of the temple and the opening of the gates to the kingdom. It is the closing of the past and the opening to the present.

But- What does a person say, when all of a sudden everything that they know and believe comes crashing down in their lives? What do you say in that moment of silence, when trust in the future is wavering? What do you say, when your will, and your hope has been shattered like a porcelain vase on a marble floor? What do you feel, when people despise your gift, when they ridicule your faith, when they have bullied you and made you feel worthless? What do you say- when all eyes are on you during the time of your weakness? What do you say - when you just simply can't take stress anymore- but you won't allow yourself to lose, nor will you allow your purpose to be shaken, and you won't allow the threats of the enemy to move you?

You cannot keep silent- you have to say something because *YOU* are the one God chose to make a difference in the life of His people. We must keep in mind the prophetic calling on the life of Jesus, the messianic calling on his life, the call of leadership, the call of shepherding.

I believe that we can all relate parishioners, preachers, and pastors- to the multipurpose fullness of the CALL- because when we think about it we are all called to something. We are called to be effective parents, teachers, family and friends, and on the other side of that coin, we all can related to the feelings of being used up – feelings of isolation, knowing that after you have prayed, cried, listened, counseled, encouraged, - some of them still don't get the point of what God has called you to do.

And there you have it... feelings of abandonment and isolation.

Let's not dismiss the fact that Jesus in his humanity was dehydrated and had lost a tremendous amount of blood. He was bruised; he was despised and ridiculed all the way to the *place of the skull*. At that moment was an articulation of suffering. Although he was suffering, he extended his voice of lament to the people who would hear. He stayed there and he preached the word of God. From the sixth to the ninth hour Jesus, the Humanity of God's word, declared the Truth of God to the people who were passing by.

Meanwhile in the temple, at the same time, the sacrifices were being bled out- cut up, blood was being poured out on the altar, - a religious atonement for the people of God, only for those who can afford to make the sacrifice – but what about the people who cannot make the sacrifice, what do we do with those who have been disinherited by racism, classism, sexism- what atonement do the people who have been rejected by the temple, and can't afford to pay the tax, they have been told that their sacrifice isn't good enough, their service isn't good enough? Jesus sums up the feeling in a simple psalm:

"God my God why have you forsaken me?" is a rallying cry for social justice. Now, I would be dismissed if I did not make mention of the historical significance of the text. First of all, it deserves to be mentioned that this famous phrase is found in Psalm 22: 1. It is thought that Jesus is calling on Elijah, which in the Jewish culture, calling on "Eli" or Elijah is a cry for help. To make my case, being that Eli is a prophet, this cry is a cry for prophetic help. Regardless of what it is interpreted as, Jesus uses his voice as a cry for help.

It is Christ in his humanity that makes this petition. He is sharing the feelings that all of his on lookers have felt. According to my Jewish New Testament Commentary- This phrase is recorded by Matthew a Jew, and when he mentions this one phrase it means that Jesus recited the entire psalm.[clvi] The Holy Spirit spoke to me and said He was preaching to the people even from the cross. He was preaching even though he was in pain. There are times in our lives that we have to preach from a place of pain. There are times that our pain is just what someone else needs to hear. When we articulate the suffering of Christ in our flesh, we reveal that the truth of our situation has a name,- that those feelings of emotions that left you feeling abandoned, and absconded, and abused can be identified… and somebody passing by needs to witness the articulation of grief turning into Joy.

Jesus articulates the suffering of God in the flesh, and he validates his authority as a King from the line of David, A Prophet from the line of Elijah, A Priest for the people, and an innocent sacrifice. By saying these words, he opens the path way for people to talk to God- because of this phrase recited by Jesus, the people no longer need to wait at the gate, or by the side of the pool, they no longer have to wait at the well, because of what Jesus said- those who had been dismissed by the higher religious societies were accepted – and gained access to God through the atoning sacrifice of Jesus.

In Psalm 22:24-26 Jesus said this on the cross- "For he has not despised or scorned the suffering of the afflicted one; he has not hidden his face from him but has listened to his cry for help. From you comes the theme of my praise in the great assembly before those who fear you I will fulfill my vows- [now] the poor will eat and be satisfied, those who seek the Lord will praise him- may your hearts live forever…"

Someone needs to hear your voice, your suffering and your story- and because of who God has created you to be, you are the one who needs to say it to those who are passing by. Even in your own place of carrying your own cross, be pleasing to God, by fulfilling your call. Pray even if you do not feel that God is listening. Listen for God's Word and truth in moments and places that you wouldn't expect to hear it. I believe that every need God will supply, but you must continue in your call- all the way to the end- and wait for the power of God to resurrect you.

Lastly, I want to share one more sermonic word of encouragement. Many of us have suffered abuse, not only physical, but spiritual and psychological abuse. How many of us have tried to prove that we are strong by dismissing it, not dealing with it, refusing to talk about it? Does this prove our strength, or does it prove that we may not trust God's strength, which is made perfect in our weakness?[clvii]

Confronting those broken places in your life is important to both your spiritual and psychological freedom and growth. In this dissertation we have talked extensively about those steps of forgiveness. It is important that we as women factor in the Truth of God so that we can get to the place where we have the freedom to be who, what, and where God designed us to be.

I do not believe that God wants us to remain broken and living in despair. I believe that God wants to reconcile those places where we have dilemmas rather than virtues. But we have to revisit those places in our lives that seem overwhelming. For us to be healed, it will mean that we will have to face situations from our pasts that seem bigger today than they were yesterday.

The Bible tells us In 2 Peter Chapter one to make every effort to align ourselves with the word of God and the gospel so that we can become bold in the ministry, so that we can add virtue through our faith, because we have the promise of God and we participate with God and we have escaped corruption. But I will admit that there are sometimes when confronting my past, the abuse, the abandonment, and the attacks have seemed as though I was like David facing Goliath.

Here is a sermon I wrote about being under pressure to face a Giant. I hope that this helps you in those times of confronting the dilemmas of your past, the situations you may be dealing with today, and courage for the challenges in your future.

6.3 Pressure to Face a Giant: A Brief Outline for Overcoming Doubt with Hope.
1 Samuel 17:37.

37 The Lord who rescued me from the paw of the lion and the paw of the bear will rescue me from the hand of this Philistine." Saul said to David, "Go, and the Lord be with you."

The battle is taking place in a battlefield near *Soch in Judah*. Being that the battlefield is in Judah, it means that the Philistines are invading the Israeli territory. Saul must respond by meeting the troops before they totally invade the territory. The Philistines were not ever able to defeat the people of God in previous battles, so they tried a different tactic this time. They wanted one on one combat, which would affirm the belief that either the gods or the stronger god would grant victory. [clviii]

In some logic this form of battle grants a win-win since individual combat would minimize casualties. Since Goliath represented the Philistine army, his height, and weaponry gave him an obvious physical advantage over his opponent. [clix] It also fed his ego as a man and warrior. Even King Saul, who is considered Israel's champion by displaying significant characteristics, is terrified as he is out heighted by Goliath.[clx] Because of Goliath's size and strength, no Israelite will challenge him.[clxi]

The commentary states that this stand-off has been going on for 40 days.[clxii] Saul the king and David's tough brothers are not up to the challenge. "When David reaches the camp, he hears Goliath defy Israel and sees Israel's soldiers run in fear. Angered, David decides to fight the giant."[clxiii] The author means for us to understand that David did not come to the battle as a warrior; he was fulfilling his family obligations and checking on his brothers. In his decision to take up Goliath's challenge, David's motives are not fame or fortune, but to honor God and remove the disgrace of Israel.[clxiv]

When we reach the scripture here, in the text, we see that at the time of this conflict there is a conversation, a conviction and then a confrontation. Lastly, the virtue to be gained here is hope and confidence in the Lord. (Alliteration)

Before I get into these three points, it is noteworthy that the prefix "Con" is a variant of com in words such as community. "Con" in its essence means together, or with. [clxv] To have a conversation means to *talk with*. It's a conviction, a firm belief, or the appearance of being convinced.[clxvi] This too requires agreement or alignment "with." And then confront, which involves more than just one's self. There must be an exchange involving more than an isolated idea or person.

Conversation:

When you are about to fight with a giant or any obstacle that is blocking your path, the bible says that it is wise to seek the counsel of the elders (ref. Luke 14:31). Often when we are facing conflict it is helpful to have a conversation with someone else. Having that conversation for mature people will do one of two things, reaffirm your beliefs or change your entire perspective. The conversation between Saul and David highlights David's courage and his faith in the living God.[clxvii]

Some conversations that people will have to give information, and to get information. By design, people will use conversations stroke your ego and others to strengthen your faith. In the process of these conversations one question I want you to ask yourself, before your get anyone's opinion, advice, compliment… have you talked with God? Have you been in the presence of the Lord? Have you had enough conversation with the almighty God so that when you get ready to go forth with what you are about to do… it is just a supplement to what God has already ordained?

There is a difference in the conversation when a person is in it to ego stroke… is that it creates an artificial relationship; an only on the surface friendship. When the thrill is gone, and they have gotten what they can get… the time is spent and the relationship takes a turn. Someone gets hurt, someone feels exploited, and nobody wins. Yet, when the conversation is faith building, it creates an intimacy and an affirming what God has for you to do. Some of us won't get that from the outside-There are some people that will never pat you on the back… that's why the Bible says that we have to esteem ourselves in the face of adversity. That's why the Lord Says, Fear not for I AM with you. That kind of conversation must come from the inside

David was beginning to feel the pressure to face a Giant. As I put myself in David's place, I began to realize that the giant he was facing was not the physical form of Goliath, but the mindset of a people who had no faith in a God who had proved himself faithful! The Giant wasn't only Goliath who had a fixed mindset and had absolutely no faith in Israel's God…. But Saul, David's brothers, and all the soldiers who has been terrorized for over a month were the giants.

David is pressured into facing a Giant.

Conviction:

When you are about to wrestle with a giant, there has to be a deep seeded conviction that what you are doing is purely for the Glory of the Lord. I understand that in battle -strategy, military strength, and armor are essential in preparation. David however in conversation affirms his conviction. He also in essence reaffirms my notion that it is not the physical nature of Goliath that he is about to destroy, because he compares Goliath to a lion or a bear. These types of enemies David has faced before. David is not intimidated by Goliath's size or strength. He has dealt with physical beasts far more fierce and violent than him. David's conviction comes because he is offended that this Man's ego has trumped everyone's faith in the God of Israel.

There is a point in time where we as mature carriers of God's word should be offended when reverence for our God is compromised by obstacles and barriers, and others who should be strong in the faith are convinced that the Giant is unable to be defeated. How is it that so many people, who have such a history with God, have forgotten so easily how strong and mighty God is? How does someone else's opinion of you, change your truth and you yield to compromise because you fear conflict? What?! Only people without a relationship with

God will tuck their tails and try to be politically correct when confronted with the ways of the world; they will shush God and accept popular opinion only because they don't want to wrestle with the twisted mindset of the world. David makes an announcement with conviction-

David makes it clear that he can defeat Goliath physically. Yet this battle is more significant to affirming glory of God, and rekindling the faith of Israel in their God, *"seeing that he [Goliath] has defiled the armies of the living God."* I cannot stress enough that this battle was not about the physical stature but the psychological mindset and influence of a people. The bible says that we wrestle not against flesh and blood, but against principalities and wickedness and evil rulers in high places (paraphrased). The Bible calls for us to cast down every vain imagination and high thing that exalts itself against the knowledge of God (paraphrased). This battle was not about defeating a physical being, but a destructive spirit of doubt.

Confrontation:

I am a firm believer that psychological mindsets can only be changed by spiritual transformation. The Bible says be not conformed to the ways of this world but be ye transformed by the renewing of your mind. You have to confront spiritual things with spiritual thing. David confronts doubt with a renewing of hope. I can see

David, as he made his way, came down from the hilltop, into the battle ground in the valley. I could see him as he was making his way picking up stones along the way. With his staff in his hand, which keeps him balanced, represents his experience and authority. I can see everyone looking over the edge to see if he would do what they had allowed themselves to be convinced not to. I can picture David in my mind, as he was making his way down the hill, reciting his songs and prayers. I can see David as he was making his way down the hill, having flashbacks of the lion and the bear, and overcoming that feeling of fear in the pit of his stomach. I can visualize through the eyes of David, a young boy, watching Goliath as he scoffed, and prided himself in his god. I can imagine that as David was aiming, he wanted to hit that *high thing* that acknowledged itself against the knowledge of God- and before he knew it, he had hit Goliath right in the head.

Not only was David confronting Goliath but I am sure he was confronting some things within himself. Predestined to be a leader, David has to return to a people who have lost hope in the God who has kept them all this time. But because of his relationship with God, David was able to speak life over himself and give all of the Glory to the God of Israel. According to research and study, Leaders who are credible and courageous, believe that they can turn the tide of negative events to their advantage while making gains for personal and societal growth. [clxviii]David acknowledged the reality but didn't spend much time dwelling on the threat. He exerted what leaders call internal control, rather than being controlled externally by what the others had to say and the events at hand. This is not to be confused with a person who has gone rogue. Let's make it clear; David had not only the authority of God, but also the affirmation and permission of the king (He was in order).

Confidence

David had a bigger Giant to face; he was facing the giant of doubt, helplessness and hopelessness. In this battle, David had to inspire hope and optimism into the people of God. He had to prove how powerful God is to the naysayers. In the face of those who were trying to invade and take over, spiritual hoarders and bullies, David was chosen to be the one who would slay this giant of a mindset that is contrary to the will and purpose of God. David was willing to share in the struggle, the anxiety, and the tension, without compromising hope. David got involved with the situation and regardless of the outcome, he confronted the giant with the will and the word of God.

Today many of us are facing giant mentality and mindsets which are contrary against the will and the word of God. Like David, some of those mindsets are external with minimal internal struggle. For others- the opinion of the giant has devastated you and your entire community. It could be like Saul, you may have jumped ahead of God and now feel that God may not be with you. Some of you may be critical of everything like David's brothers and are so pessimistic that you have killed your own ability to hope in God. Some of you may be like the crowd, not really knowing what's real you have been disappointed by leadership and don't know what to believe or where to put your faith. Some of you have been tormented for 40 days, 40 months, and even 40 years by an opinion of the world, and for so long you haven't had enough courage to speak God's word over your life… well today, I'm going to be like David, I am going to take the first step to begin defeating those giants and bringing those high things into captivity with the world of God. Let's picture ourselves as David, I wrote down a few verses that will jump start us when we are under pressure to face a giant starting with:

- 1 John 4:4-Greater is the God in me than the God who is in the world.

- Psalm 27: 1-3 - The Lord is my light and my salvation, whom shall I fear? The Lord is the strength of my life, of whom shall I be afraid? When my enemies and my foes came to eat up my flesh… they stumbled and fell. Even though I have this giant in front and naysayers and spectators behind me (paraphrased "encamped")

… My heart shall not fear…

- Psalm 28: 7- the Lord is my strength and my shield, my heart trusted in him and I am helped…

My dear sister, as I close this conversation. I pray that you have been strengthened. Keep in mind that one of the most important steps regarding our growth in God is that we make a conscious decision to develop our self-esteem (our self- image) in God. In order to do that; we must desire to model the character of God and think differently about ourselves (as far as our ability, strength, weakness, etc). I was talking to a friend on the phone one day and she revealed something to me in a way that I could fully understand, she said to me, "When you know what you are worth [for yourself] then you don't need anyone to build your esteem."

The Bible says, 'Let this mind be in you that is also in Christ Jesus" (Phil 2:5). This means that in our walk with God there should be a transformation in our minds and thoughts including the ones we have about ourselves. I believe that each of us will experience a time when we will have to define ourselves in God, apart from our roles in our relationships with individuals, the Church, or in ministry. That will be the time that we will grow, heal, and have the power to help someone- because knowing our identity in God and seeing ourselves the way that God sees us is the most important part of our growth experience with God. This is a decision that we must make daily; to choose to see ourselves as God sees us. I am a firm believer that when we engage God, in worship, we find that our voice is his voice, our words are his words, our stories are his stories- redeemed, reconciled, recovered and revived.

6.4 Go in Peace, Your Faith has Saved You.

"And He said to her, Daughter your faith Has made you well, Go in Peace and be healed of your affliction"

. I want to tell you a story about a desperate woman, a helpless man, and an overwhelmed generation. This Story takes place in the shorelines of Galilee called Gerasa. As this sermon evolved from Last Monday, I had to know and understand what was going on in this territory to make this story come alive. This place had suffered devastation and trauma, because Roman soldiers had invaded it at least one to two generations before Christ visited this territory.

Broken Pieces

How can anything broken be made whole, or how can something sick be made well? To make something whole, suggests to me that there must have been something broken at one time or another and there is a process of restoration which must take place. In this text we see a lot of broken pieces. It is my hope to illustrate for you in this story how we can use faith to make us not only well, but whole!

In this territory, we have a man tormented by a legion of demons and was cutting himself in the graveyard. This action showed severe signs of depression and disorientation due to a traumatic event that has happened in the life of this community. When Jesus asked him, "what is happening with you, put a name on your condition" the man replies, "Legion" which in fact represents a unit of 3,000 – 6,000 men in a roman army. It sets the stage for the remaining story because this man was not able to pinpoint any one thing that happened to him to cause this response to the immediate dilemma of his society. Something had been happening here for generations.

The Helpless Men

In this territory Jesus is constantly met with the psychological problems of the men.

1) A demon possessed man who has lost everything and is now cutting himself in the tombs.

2) was the Centurion, who's servant was sick- confirming the Roman presence and the relationship dynamic in the territory. It is a man

who understands authority, and yet has no authority over the sickness of his servant.

3) The Paralyzed Young man and his friends (Matthew Chapter 9)

4) The Two Blind Men.

5) The Mute Man: A Man with No VOICE.

6) The Father and His Demon Possessed Son

7) Then we have the religious leader of the local synagogue, whose daughter is sick.

He is one of the people in this territory who is dealing with all of the generational trauma of this community- imagine the burden it is putting on him and his family. He represents the religious leaders of the society who has probably been trying to care for the psychological issues of the area he serves, and now he is having trouble in his own home. He is dealing with multiple generations of traumatized men and their families, and he is helpless to deal with it all. It has gotten so bad that it has affected his own household. He naturally is one of the first to meet Jesus when he arrives. I say this because as a religious leader we have to be the ones to bring our concerns first. Yet this situation also represents how easy and how often our requests are interrupted and seemingly delayed, but I

want to encourage you leaders, when this happens-
"ONLY BELIEVE." Keep the faith.

CAN YOU SEE THE CROWD?

The status of this generation and community is so dire
that people begin to press into Jesus, as soon as they hear
that he has arrived. I can only imagine that their needs
have been neglected for so long- I can imagine them
calling out to Jesus Trying to get his attention.

I can visualize the local religious leader who is now so
focused on the survival of his own house trying to pull
Jesus through the crown.

I can see that they keep having to stop because the streets
begin to fill up with people, as the news spreads through
the town that a healer has arrived there.

Suddenly there is a woman who pulls at the cloak of
Jesus. She is so desperate for healing that she pulls from
the bottom. Her posture, not only her physical posture,
but her spiritual and psychological posture pulls the
virtue from his body. In this text the virtue is the same as
power. What gives us power? Hope, Will, a sense of
purpose and understanding, faithfulness and love, caring
for ourselves and others, and last but not least, wisdom.
This woman was in such need of that kind of power that
her pull on the anointing of Jesus made him stop and take
notice of the Hopeless women

The Hopelessness of the Women

The first psychological crisis that any person must resolve is the crisis of trust versus mistrust. The virtue to be gained from resolving that dilemma is hope. The issue that this hemorrhaging woman, as well as Jairus' daughter represent here is the same: it is that they have been marginalized by a society which was unsympathetic to the emotional needs of the women. These two women were displaying normal signs of what we call the "Father Complex," or "Daddy Issues."

The Daddy Issue in psychology points to the psychological issues a girl has when she is rejected by her father or is a result from the absenteeism of the father. In addition, any other type of abnormal relations or relationship with the father manifests in a distrust of or sexual desire for men who act as father figures. These women have trouble finding a significant other. They yearn for the protection and validation of a male figure.

This hemorrhaging woman is a part of the current culture and generation of working-class women amongst a helpless society of men who have suffered and endured severe trauma, resulting in absent fathers due to incarceration by the roman government- or the local mental institution. A government which has a desensitized view of the poor. A Health care industry that is more concerned with the kickbacks they get from the pharmaceutical companies than education and preventative care. She lives in a religious society which is on the decline in its attendance, due to the fact that the leaders are currently experiencing compassion fatigue because the issues of society are now creeping in to their living rooms.

The Pastors Child

The Pastor's daughter represents the next generation of life, and she is overwhelmed to the point of death. How is she going to carry the responsibility of being a wife and a mother to a family when she doesn't even know the love of her absent father? She needs validation, and assurance. She is at the age where so much is expected of her. She is 12 years old and for some reason she is surrounded by a crowd of people who are expecting her to be something she is not ready to be. She is at the age "where daughters would be offered by their fathers in marriage to other men's sons, who were normally a few years older" (Donald Capps, 2008, 113). She was expected to become a woman and assume all the responsibilities that womanhood entailed" (ibid). Yet she was not psychologically nor emotionally ready for that responsibility- she is 12 years old and still a little girl. Studies have proven that there is a severe psychological disorientation in connection to sexual activity with women who are not psychologically or emotionally ready for it. The act and the anxiety is traumatizing. Whatever had happened to her put her into a place of hysteria, which was associated with a death like trance.

We don't know why, we don't know the details, but what we do know is that she is experiencing what psychologist call **Undifferentiated Somatoform Disorder.** Both of these women have shown some kind of signs and symptoms. They have so much anxiety, their needs have been severely neglected, they need the love of a father figure, but all of the men are helpless to meet the need.

The women in this story are desperate from age 12 to about 46 years old. *It would seem that the whole entire city has lost its Faith and is looking for a word of Truth and Hope.*

What does Jesus Do?

The Bible tells us in this story that there is something going on deeper than what the eyes can see, *(and if you stay with me, I promise that we are all going to be helped and healed today.)

What happens when Jesus shows up?

1) He's a Man (Physically)

2) He's a Man of God (Spiritually)

3) He's a figure of Authority (Power)

4) He has his own business (carpenter/ handyman), which means he has his own money, tax accountant, security.

5) He Knows the Word of God!

If I was one of those women in that territory with all of those broken men, I would probably be in the crowd too. Everyone had a different reason that they wanted to get to Jesus.

But what Jesus does is very important:

- Rather than preach the curse of the law, he proclaims the blessings of Faith.
- He speaks life to the ones who have sentenced themselves to death.
- He speaks truth to those who have been taught to believe a lie.
- He reveals purpose to those who feel guilty about their life story.
- He initiates acceptance to those who have been cast out of society simply because the majority chose not to deal with the infirmities of those they refused to understand.

Jesus Answers it all-

"As the woman approached Jesus in fear and trembling, fell down before him and told him the whole truth, he called her 'Daughter'." While her touch of his cloak eliminated the symptoms, his words to her made her well and whole. He showed her tenderness. Jesus had taken the role of the Father in this woman's life- when she told him everything- the buried and forgotten love she had transferred onto Jesus were for her own father, but for some reason she had not received the proper recognition or response. She was looking for the appropriate love from a father figure. Jairus, witnessed this act of love from a **father like figure.**

When he takes the little girl by the hand, he had sent everyone who did not believe her, everyone who did not want to listen to her out of the room. He listened to her, he listened to her fears, he listened to her needs, and he addressed her as she needed to be addressed at the time, rather than saying WOMAN, which was the expectation for her, he says "little girl". He restores her innocence- He has compassion. In compassion there is power.

Jesus stepped in as a surrogate for another man.

Romans 8:15 (NLT) "So you have not received a spirit that makes you fearful slaves. Instead, you received God's Spirit when he adopted you as his own children. Now we call him, "Abba, Father."

NOT ONLY were the women healed, but the men who took the example from Jesus. Any of the men who learned how to listen with compassion to the women and be present in their daughter's lives without exploiting them or abusing them became representatives of hope in these women's lives. This is the power of true and authentic love.

"Daughter, Go In peace, your faith has made you whole."

Now, Jesus says that since all power was given to me, and I am giving that same power to you. Go and do likewise, making disciples and teaching them everything that I have taught you to do.

6.5 I hope this has helped.

I encourage you to get into the word of so that you can understand the truth about yourself even more. I encourage you, do not allow the enemy to hold you in a state of self-condemnation one more minute. Saturate yourself in true and authentic worship. Begin to embrace your story. Embrace the truth about your life and who God says that you are. I encourage you to begin to realize that everything you have been through in your life has brought you to this point where you can have the skill and the courage slay the giants of your past. Find the needs that have left voids in your life and use your voice to have them met. Identify yourself, apart from your role in your current relationships, and functions, from your title, your social location, your suffering, and the list can go on and on. Are you moving toward the Truth in such a way that it tips the scales from forsaken to forgiven?

Don't settle with the suggestions from the mental institutions and labeling systems that make you believe that you are unworthy to receive the gospel of Jesus Christ. Don't let the memories of what you used to be, or what you used to do- hold you hostage any longer ... use your tragedy as a testimony of what God can do with a sinner, what God can do with a persecutor, what God can do with a person just like you, designed by him for just a time as this. Unshackle yourself.

Today I encourage you to let this be the day to begin to receive the abundance of blessing in a relationship with Christ. I invite you to read one last sermon if you are feeling doubtful about the purpose of God in your life. You may have feelings of tremendous pressure. Let me remind you that God is standing up for you, in you and with you; because to God - you are worth it!

Bibliography

Alexander, Michelle. *The New Jim Crow: Mass Incarceration in the Age of Colorblindness.* New York: The New Press, 2012.

Barnes Lampman , Lisa, ed. *God and the Victim: Theological Reflections on Evil, Victimization, Justice and Forgiveness.* Grand Rapids : Eerdmans Publishing, 1999.

Brengle, Samuel L. *The Guest Of the Soul .* Noblesville, IN: Newby Book Room, 1971.

Brueggemann, Walter. *The Message of the Psalms: A Theological Commentary.* Minneapolis: Augsburg Press, 1984.

Crough, Patrick. *The Serpents Among Us: How to Protect Your Children From Sexual Predators.* Rochester: Millstone Justice, 2009.

Dawn, Marva J. *Reaching Out Without Dumbing Down: A Theology of Worship for This Urgent Time.* Grand Rapids: Eerdmans, 1995.

Donna, Allen Eleanor. *Toward a Womanist Homiletic: Katie Cannon and Alice Walker, An Emancipatory Proclaimation.* Nashville: Vanderbilt University, 2005.

In *A Troubling in My Soul: Womanist Perspectives On Evil and Suffering*, by Ed. Emilie M. Townes. Maryknoll, NY: Orbis Books, 1993.

Evans, Mandy. *Traveling Free: How to Recover from the Past by Changing Your Beliefs*. Desert Hot Springs: Yes You Can Press, 1990.

Hollies, Linda H. *Inner Healing for Broken Vessels: Seven Steps to a Woman's way of Healing* . Nashville : Upperroom books, 1992.

House, Paul R., Mitchell Eric. *Old Testament Survey: 2nd Edition* . Nashville: B & H Publishing Group, 2007.

Kaiser, Walter C. *Preaching and Teaching from the Old Testament: A Guide for the Church.* Grand Rapids: Baker Books, 2003.

Kouzes, James M., and Barry Z. Posner. *Credibility: Why Leaders Gain and Lose It, Why People Demand It.* San Francisco : Jossey- Bass, 2003.

McClure, John S. *Other Wise Preaching: A Postmodern Ethic for Homiletics* . St. Louis, MO: Chalice Press , 2001.

MCMickle, Marvin A. *Be My Witness: The Great Commission for Preachers.* Valley Forge: Judson Press, 2016.

"New Bible Commentary: 21 Century Edition." Downers Grove: Intervarsity Press , 1994.

Newbigin, Lesslie. *The Gospel in a Pluralist Society.* Grand Rapids, MI: Eerdmans Publishing, 1989.

Oden, Thomas C,. *After Modernity...What?* Grand Rapids: Zondervan, 1990.

Stern, David. *New Jewish Commentary*. Clarksville: Jewish New Testament Publications, 1989.

Townes, Emilie M. *Womanist Ethics and the Cultural Production of Evil.* New York: Palgrave Macmillan, 2006.

---

[i] Ann Olson, "The Theory of Self-Actualization Mental illness, creativity and art," Psychology Today, August 13, 2013, accessed September 30, 2017, http://www.psychologytoday.com/blog/theory-and-psychopathology/201308/the-theory-self-actualization. Olson also notes that "Carl Rogers created a theory implicating a 'growth potential' whose aim was to integrate congruently the 'real self' and the 'ideal self' thereby cultivating the emergence of the 'fully functioning person.'"

[ii] Genesis 19:30-38 (NKJV).

[iii] *New Bible Commentary, 21st Century Edition* (Downers Grove: Intervarsity Press 1994), 75.

[iv] Ibid., 75

[v] Ibid., 75

[vi] *Women's Bible Commentary: Twentieth Anniversary Edition*, eds. Carol A. Newsome, Sharon H. Ringe, Jacqueline E. Lapsley, 3rd Ed. (Louisville: Westminster Knox, 2012).

[vii] Trible, "Feminist," 156.

[viii] Emilie M. Townes, *Womanist Ethics and the Cultural Production of Evil* (New York: Palgrave MacMillan, 2006), 4.

[ix] "Truth" capitalized as a personification of God.

[x] Black and African American used interchangeably.

[xi] Carolyn McCray, "The Wholeness of Women," *Journal of the Interdenominational Theological Center*, 25 no. 3, Spring 1998, 258-294.

[xii] Carolyn Akua L. McCrary, "Intimate Violence Against Black Women and Internalized Shame: A Womanist Pastoral Counseling Perspective," *Journal of Interdenominational Theological Center* 28, no. 1–2 (Fall-Spring 2000–2001): 3-37. From Atlanta, Georgia, Dr. McCrary was the visiting scholar in the Womanist Scholars Program, Office of Black Women in Church and Society, ITC, during her sabbatical for the 2000-2001 academic years. Presented in ITC chapel on March 29, 2001.

[xiii] Ibid.

[xiv] Ibid.

[xv] Barbara A. Holmes, (Farmington Hills, Michigan: The Gale Group Inc. 2003). Http://www.encyclopedia.com. (Published under license from the publisher through the Gale Group. All inquiries regarding rights should be directed to the Gale Group)

[xvi] Ibid.

[xvii] Ibid.

[xviii] Toinette M. Eugene, *There is a Balm in Gilead: Black Women and the Black Church as Agents of a Therapeutic Community,* quoted in *Women and Therapy* 1995: no.16, 2-3 (Evanston, IL: Hawthorn Press, 1995), 56.

[xix] Deloris S. Williams, "Womanist Theology: Black Women's Voices" *Christianity and Crisis*, March 2, 1987, accessed September 24, 2015, http://www.religion-online.org/article/womanist-theology-black-womens-voices.

[xx] Ibid.

[xxi] Ibid.

[xxii] Ibid

[xxiii] Ibid.

[xxiv] William H. Willimon, *The Intrusive Word: Preaching to the Unbaptized* (Grand Rapids: Eerdmans Publishing, 1994), 35-39.

[xxv] Thomas C. Oden, *After Modernity...What?: Agenda for Theology* (Grand Rapids: Zondervan Publishing, 1990), 74.

[xxvi] Glossary of Theological Terms in *The Christian Theology Reader 3rd Edition* (Malden, MA: Blackwell Publishing,

2007), Ed. Alister E. McGrath, *s.v.* Postmodern.

[xxvii] TbPSD- Trauma based Psycho-spiritual Disorientation.

[xxviii] Phyllis Trible, "On Feminist Biblical Interpretation," in *The Christian Theology Reader*, 3rd ed., ed. Alister E. McGrath (Malden, MA: Blackwell Publishing, 2007), 157.

[xxix] Mandy Evans, *Traveling Free: How to Recover from the Past by Changing Your Beliefs* (Desert Hot Springs, CA: Yes You Can Press, 1990), 47.

[xxx] Benjamin B. Lahey, *Psychology: An Introduction*, Seventh ed. (New York: McGraw Hill Publishing, University of Chicago, 2001) 610.

[xxxi] Ibid., 610.

[xxxii] Michelle Alexander, *The New Jim Crow: Mass Incarceration in the Age of Colorblindness* (New York, New Press Publishing: 2012), 166.

[xxxiii] Consubstantial Definition: "Of one and the same substance or being. The word is used esp. of the eternal relationship which subsists between the three Persons of the Holy Trinity." *Oxford Dictionary of the Christian Church, Third Edition* (New York: Oxford University Press, 1997), s.v. Consubstantial.

[xxxiv] Pam Nugent, *Psychology Dictionary*, https://psychologydictionary.org/?s=disorientation April 7, 2013, (accessed March 21, 2017).

[xxxv] Walter, Brueggemann, *The Message of the Psalms: A Theological Commentary* (Augsburg: Minneapolis, 1984), 51.

[xxxvi] Ananya Mandal, MD., "Hippocampus Functions", *News Medical Life Sciences,* January 14, 2014, Https://www.news-medical.net/health/hippocampus-functions.aspx. (accessed, January 11, 2018).

[xxxvii] James R. Phelps MD., "Memory, Learning and Emotion: the Hippocampus" on *PsychEducation.org: Treating the Mood Spectrum,* December 2014, http://www.psycheduation.org/brain-tours/memory-learning-and-emotion-the-hippocampus/ (accessed January 11, 2018)

[xxxviii] What Causes Depression?", an article on *Harvard Health*

Publishing, Original Publishing June 2009, Updated April 11, 2017, https://www.health.harvard.edu/mind-and-mood/what-causes-depression (accessed January 20, 2019).

xxxix Ibid.

xl James Phelps, Ibid.

xli Ibid.

xlii Ibid.

xliii See Chapter 6.6

xliv National Childhood Sexual Abuse Statistics, https://victimsofcrime.org (N.d), (accessed March 11, 2015).

xlv Ibid.

xlvi Brueggemann, *Message of the Psalms,* 52.

xlvii Saul McLoed, "Carl Rogers," in *Simply Psychology, 2014,* https://www.simplypsychology.org/carl-rogers.html (accessed November 14, 2015).

xlviii Melissa and Joshua Hall, *Long Term Consequences of Child Sexual Abuse, In* "Ideas and Research You Can Use: VISTAS 2011." American Counseling Association, https://www.counseling.org/docs/disaster-and-trauma_sexual-abuse/long-term-effects-of-childhood-sexual-abuse.pdf?sfvrsn=2 (accessed May, 20th 2016).

xlix Ibid.

l Ibid.

li *Child Sexual Abuse Statistics*, at https://www.d2l.org/wp-content/uploads/2017/01/all_statistics_20150619.pdf. www.darknesstolight.org (accessed June 13, 2016).

lii Finklehor, et al 1990, as cited on "Child Abuse Research and Statistics," www.prevent-abuse-now.com/stats.htm (accessed June 17, 2016).

liii Ibid.

liv Ibid.

lv Larry K. Brown, M.D., et al, American Journal of Psychiatry, 2000: 157:1413-1415 at https://ajp.psychiatryonline.org/ (accessed on May 23, 2016).

lvi Ibid.

lvii www.darknesstolight.org

lviii Ibid.

lix Jerman J, Jones RK and Onda T, *Characteristics of U.S. Abortion*

Patients in 2014 and Changes Since 2008 (New York: Guttmacher Institute, 2016) on https://www.guttmacher.org/fact-sheet/state-facts-about-abortion-new-york. January 2018 fact sheet (accessed January 13, 2018)
[lx] Ibid.
[lxi] Kenneth S. Kendler, M.D., et al, Medical College of Virginia Common Wealth University, Archives of General Psychiatry 2000;57:953-959. Cited on www.prevent-abuse-now.com/stats.htm (accessed June 17,2016)
[lxii] Finkler and Browne, 1986 as cited in "Research Archives of Noteworthy Findings: Child Sexual Abuse –Disclosures," on www.prevent-abuse-now.com/stats.htm (accessed June 11, 2016)
[lxiii] Cathy Spatz Windom, "Victims of Childhood Sexual Abuse Later Criminal Consequences," March 1995 cited on *Child Abuse Research and Statistics,* www.prevent-abuse-now.com/stats.htm.
[lxiv] Kirsten Beronio, Rosa Po, Laura Skopec, Sherry Glied, "Affordable care act Expands mental health and substance abuse disorder benefits and federal parity protections for 62 Million Americans" Published 02/20/2013 on U.S Department of health & Human Services; Office of the Assistant Secretary for Planning and Evaluation. at https://aspe.hhs.gov/report (Accessed June 13th 2014).
[lxv] Ibid.
[lxvi] Ibid.
[lxvii] Benjamin B Lahey, *Psychology: An Introduction*, 7th ed. (New York: McGraw-Hill Publishing, 2001), 536-561.
[lxviii] Ibid.

[lxix] Ibid.
[lxx] Ibid.
[lxxi] Randy J. Nelson has two PhDs (Psychology and Endocrinology) and is Professor and Chair of Neuroscience and Professor of Psychology at The Ohio State University. He has been appointed as University Distinguished Professor for his work on hormones, biological rhythms, and behavior. Dr. Nelson has published nearly 400 papers and several books on these topics.
[lxxii] Randy J. Nelson, *Hormones and Behavior,* in R. Biswas-Diener & E. Diener (Eds), Noba textbook series: Psychology (Champaign, IL: DEF publishers, 2018) DOI:nobaproject.com (accessed January 12,2018)

[lxxiii] Ibid.

[lxxiv]Society for Endocrinology, "Cortisol," *You and Your Hormones: An Education Resource from the Society of Endocrinology*, https:// http://www.yourhormones.info/hormones/cortisol/ January 2017. (Accessed January 12, 2018.)

[lxxv] Lahey, Psychology, 2001.

[lxxvi] Lahey, *Psychology,* 2001.

[lxxvii] Ibid., 546.

[lxxviii] Ibid.

[lxxix] Ibid.

[lxxx] Penny Cannon, Mary K Scribner, *Adult Development and Lifelong Learning: Adult Learners Guide*, Roberts Wesleyan College, July 2006. 54-56.

[lxxxi] Ibid.

[lxxxii] Ibid.

[lxxxiii] Ibid.

[lxxxiv] Ibid.

[lxxxv] See figure 2 in this document.

[lxxxvi] Ibid.

[lxxxvii] Ibid.

[lxxxviii] Lahey, *Psychology*, 2001.

[lxxxix] Mandy Evans, *Traveling Free,* 1990.

[xc] Oxford Dictionary, Oxford University Press. https://en.oxforddictionaries.com/ s.v. Reconciliation, (Accessed October 25, 2016).

[xci] Radzik, Linda and Murphy, Colleen, "Reconciliation", *The Stanford Encyclopedia of Philosophy* (summer 2015 Edition), Edward N. Zalta (ed.), https://plato.stanford.edu/archives/sum2015/entries/reconciliation. (accessed March 13,2016)

[xcii] Http://www.investopedia .com/terms/r.reconciliation.asp

[xciii] Ibid.

[xciv] I say this with the understanding that forgiveness can happen without reconciliation.

[xcv] The Stanford Encyclopedia of Philosophy, See Citation 52.

[xcvi] L. Gregory Jones, "Behold, I Make All Things New," in

God *and the Victim: Theological Reflections on Evil, Victimization, Justice and Forgiveness*, ed. Lisa Barnes Lampman and Michelle D. Shattuck (Grand Rapids, MI: William B. Eerdmans Publishing, 1999), 160-182.

[xcvii] Radzik, Linda and Murphy, Colleen, "Reconciliation", The Stanford Encyclopedia of Philosophy (Summer 2015 Edition), Edward N. Zalta (ed.) (accessed March 13, 2016).

[xcviii] Jones, *Behold,* 169-170.

[xcix] Ibid.

[c] Ibid.

[ci] Jones, *Behold,* 169- 170.

[cii] Truth is capitalized to emphasize its importance and personification.

[ciii] Jones, *Behold,* 169-170.

[civ] Ibid.

[cv] Ibid.

[cvi]James Forbes, *The Holy Spirit and Preaching* (Nashville, TN: Abingdon Press, 1989), 37.

[cvii] McClure, *Otherwise Preaching,* 74.

[cviii] Newbigin, *Pluralist Society,* 21.

[cix] McClure, *Otherwise,* 91.

[cx] McClure, 91.

[cxi] McClure, 91.

[cxii] McClure, 92.

[cxiii] Ibid.

[cxiv] McClure, *Otherwise,* 90.

[cxv] James Forbes, *Holy Spirit,* 19.

[cxvi] My own conclusive thoughts

[cxvii]Ibid.

[cxviii] James Forbes, 22.

[cxix] Oden, *After Modernity,* 1990, 177

[cxx] Tionette M. Eugene, *Balm,* 1995.

[cxxi] Ibid.

[cxxii] Walter C. Kaiser Jr., *Preaching and Teaching from the Old Testament: A Guide for the Church* (Grand Rapids: Baker Books, 2003), 113.

[cxxiii] Ibid.

[cxxiv] This five-stage model can be divided into deficiency

needs and growth needs. The first four levels are often referred to as deficiency needs (D-needs), and the top level is known as growth or being needs (B-needs). According to Samuel McLeod's Maslow's Hierarchy of Needs, which is the same as Hierarchy of Self-actualization, 2016 article on https://www.simplypsychology.org/maslow.html (accessed March, 19, 2016).

[cxxv] Images provided by Thedailyomnivore.net (Erickson), and Simplypsychology.org (Maslow)

[cxxvi] Referring to Erickson's Theory.

[cxxvii] Maslow's Theory, 1962 ref citation 138.

[cxxviii] Ibid.

[cxxix] Kaiser, *Preaching,* 2003, 117.

[cxxx] Walter Brueggemann, *Message of the Psalms: A Theological Commentary* (Minneapolis: Augsburg, 1984), 51.

[cxxxi] Ibid., 52.

[cxxxii] Ibid., 53.

[cxxxiii] Bee, H.L & Bjorklund, B.R. *The Journey of Adulthood,* 5th *ed,* Erik Erikson, "Theories of Adult Development," (Upper Saddle River, NJ: Prentice Hall, 2004), 30-53.

[cxxxiv] Mandy Evans, *Traveling Free: How to Recover from the Past by Changing Your Beliefs* (Desert Hot Springs, CA: Yes You Can Press, 1990), 47.

[cxxxv] Toinette M. Eugene, "There is A Balm in Gilead: Black Women and The Black Church as Agents of a Therapeutic Community," in *Women & Therapy,* 16:2-3 (1995), 55-69.

[cxxxvi] Ibid.

[cxxxvii] Ibid.

[cxxxviii] Pappenheim was actually treated by Freud's friend and mentor Josef Breuer. This information is from an article "Bertha Pappenheim (1859-1936) The Original Patient of Psychoanalysis" in *Psychology Today.* January 29, 2012 by Mikkel Borch-Jacobsen PhD (accessed October 23, 2016).

[cxxxix] Pam MS, NCSP, at http://psychologydictionary.org/talking-cure/ (accessed October 24, 2016)

[cxl] Stephen L. Salter, "Return of the Talking Cure: Finding the words for Chronic Pain," in *Psychology Today,* May 23, 2013.

https://www.psychologytoday.com/blog/ideals-in-question/201305/return-the-talking-cure (Accessed January 12, 2017)

[cxli] Ibid.

[cxlii] Joan Burgess Winfrey, "Pastoral Care for Abused Women," in *Women Abuse and the Bible: How Scripture can be Used to Hurt or Heal*, ed. Catherine Clark Kroeger & James R. Beck (Grand Rapids: Baker Books Publishing, 1996), 148-160.

[cxliii] T. Eugene, *Balm,* 1995.

[cxliv] Rick Meyer, *Through the Fire: Spiritual Restoration for Adult Victims of Childhood Sexual Abuse* (Minneapolis, MN: Augsburg Books, 2005), 61-71.

[cxlv] Oppression, in the spiritual context, causes emotional and spiritual bondage after a physically traumatic episode. Therefore, an oppressor is an individual who exercises his or her authority in a cruel or abusive manner, to those which are determined to be weaker, and easily victimized.

[cxlvi] Julia Watts. 65-67. Quietism definition, (in the Christian faith): devotional contemplation and abandonment of the will as a form of religious mysticism. It is the calm acceptance of things as they are without attempts to resist or change them.

[cxlvii] Translation from *Berean Study Bible*

[cxlviii] These include and are not limited to the various kinds of abuses and the long term and immediate effects of an individual who has been subjected to a domestically abusive situation. The challenge for the survivor of abuse is making God's forgiveness and reconciliation more of a reality in his or her everyday living. Not only the victim needs the assistance of a therapeutic response offered by the church, but the abuser's behavior needs to be addressed too.

[cxlix] L. Gregory Jones, "Behold, I Make All Things New," in *God and the Victim: Theological Reflections on Evil, Victimization, Justice and Forgiveness*, ed. Lisa Barnes Lampman and Michelle D. Shattuck (Grand Rapids: William B. Eerdmans Publishing, 1999), 160-182.

[cl] Therefore, trainings offered by the Church would need to teach about how abuse has been addressed historically and Biblically in order to gain a full theological perspective. Then assist the survivor into an atmosphere of worship, which will aid in reaching a level of reconciliation, and forgiveness. In addition, the perpetrator

will need teaching about taking responsibility for abusive actions and accountability for moving toward change.

[cli] James Forbes, *Holy Spirit,* 25.

[clii] McClure, *Other Wise,* 108.

[cliii] Patrick Crough, *The Serpents Among Us: How to Protect Your Children from Sexual Predators* (Rochester, NY: Millstone Justice, 2009), 49.

[cliv] Marva J. Dawn, *Reaching Out Without Dumbing Down: A Theology of Worship for this Urgent Time* (Grand Rapids: Eerdmans Publishing, 1995), 81.

[clv] Ibid, 83.

[clvi] David Stern, *New Testament Jewish Commentary* (Clarksville: Jewish New Testament Publications, 1989).

[clvii] 1 Corinthians 12: 8-10

[clviii] *New Bible Commentary, 21 Century Ed.* (Downers Grove: Inter-Varsity Press, 1994), 312-313.

[clix] Ibid.

[clx] *New Bible Commentary.*

[clxi] Paul R. House & Eric Mitchell, *Old Testament Survey: 2nd Edition* (Nashville: B &H Publishing Group, 2007), 128- 131.

[clxii] *New Bible Commentary.1994*

[clxiii] *Old Testament Survey.*

[clxiv] NBC

[clxv] http://www.dictionary.com/browse/con-

[clxvi] Ibid., conviction.

[clxvii] *New Bible Commentary,*1994.

[clxviii] James M. Kouzes & Barry Z. Posner, *Credibility; How Leaders Gain and Lose it, Why People Demand It* (San Francisco; Jossey-Bass, 2003.), 224- 229.

Made in the
USA
Columbia, SC